MARY STUART

MARY STUART

freely translated

and adapted from

Schiller's play

by

STEPHEN SPENDER

New Haven and New York

TICKNOR & FIELDS

1980

First published in the USA in 1980 by
Ticknor & Fields

Published in Great Britain in 1959 by
Faber and Faber Limited

Mary Stuart is fully protected by copyright. Application for all performing
rights in the play should be addressed to the author's agent, Margaret Ramsey,
Ltd., 14A Goodwin's Court, London, W.C.2. No performance may take place
unless a licence has been obtained.

Library of Congress Cataloging in Publication Data
Schiller, Johann Christoph Friedrich von, 1759–1805.
  Mary Stuart.
  First published under title: Schiller's Mary Stuart.
  1. Mary Stuart, Queen of the Scots, 1542–1587—
Drama. I. Spender, Stephen, 1909– II. Title.
PT2473.M3S6 1980 832'.6 79-25615
ISBN 0-89919-008-1
ISBN 0-89919-013-8 pbk.

Printed in the United States of America

V 10 9 8 7 6 5 4 3 2 1

PREFACE TO THE
AMERICAN EDITION

Mary Stuart is written for two great women stars. Mary Stuart and Queen Elizabeth. This version, which I wrote for performance at the Edinburgh Festival in September 1958, had those in Irene Worth and Catherine Lacey. The play was brilliantly directed by Peter Wood and had luxuriant costumes and scenery by Leslie Hurry. After the Festival it ran in repertory for several months at the Old Vic, where, with a different cast, it was revived some years later. There has also been a short season at the Lincoln Center in New York.

The central scene of the play is the glorious row between the two Queens, in Act III, scene iv. After a few minutes of courtesies, they rail at one another like fishwives. Schiller is very successful here in conveying the duplicity of Mary which at least equals that of Elizabeth in later scenes. Mary is wronged, humiliated, full of pathos, and yet her vow that if Elizabeth grants her freedom, she will cease to plot against her is worthless. Left alive Mary will never cease to be a schemer surrounded by infatuated fanatics yearning to die for her. Elizabeth is right to reject her, though her way of doing so reveals a passionate desire for vengeance which dramatically is a form of injustice.

Historically, of course, Elizabeth and Mary never met. The great scene which is the core of Schiller's drama never took place. Yet it shows great historic perception in that Mary and Elizabeth were obsessed with one another. Neither was ever very far from the other's thoughts. Mary was at the mercy of Elizabeth, but in a sense too, as long as this Papist French-educated Queen of Scotland lived, Elizabeth, as far as her peace of mind was concerned, was at Mary's mercy. Their thoughts and feelings were constantly in communication, and Schiller has clothed them in words. He has given a vivid portrait of Elizabeth as a schemer and powerful monarch who was also tormented herself and tormenting to others through her indecision. Mary is also a plotter but a self-destructive one. Above all she is a victim of her own passions.

The most melodramatic, and therefore to us, the least convincing role in the play, is that of Mortimer, the self-appointed rescuer of Mary by means of an absurd plot. At first sight Mortimer seems introduced into the play as a piece of machinery in order to facilitate the dénouement. Yet though seeming a figure of cardboard in himself he is convincing as an emanation of Mary's psychology. He is a composite ghost risen from her own past of lustful and murderous lovers, Bothwell and Rizzio. He embodies fantasies and temptations to which she gave way, and which Elizabeth, even while toying with them, kept at flirtatious arm's length. Elizabeth feels both contemptuous and jealous of Mary. Elizabeth is the woman who uses her femininity to gain power over others, Mary the woman who incites men on to rape her. Mortimer then, a projected fantasy of Mary, a spectre from her past, should perhaps be played almost as a lustful ghost.

The other men, Leicester, Burley, Talbot, Davison, are supporting figures to the two Queens, but they nevertheless represent attitudes and cartoons which are clearly delineated and can be strongly played.

The present translation is only about half of that which I prepared for the Old Vic, and that half has been considerably rewritten in the course of production. I have added perhaps two hundred lines which were not used for the Old Vic performance, so as to give future producers a certain freedom of choice.

Peter Wood, in addition to making cuts, has transposed some scenes and made other alterations. As Peter Wood himself put it in a preface he wrote for the English edition: "To the purist these measures may seem disrespectful but I needed to re-angle the interest of Schiller's play to develop more fully something which was there in the original, but which was blanketed for an English audience by a mass of history and rhetorical melodrama."

So the original German text of Schiller is a marble block out of which translator and producer have hewn a work suitable for a non-German English-language audience. A German producer who saw the Old Vic performance told me that this version was not so much a translation as a series of poetic variations on themes provided by Schiller, like the work of some modern composer founded on a theme of Bach. I would take it as a compliment if I thought this were really so. More modestly, I would say it is a streamlined adaptation modified in the course of rehearsals in the interests of making a play that is a self-contained actable unity. What Irene Worth, Catherine Lacey and the other members of the caste, and Peter Wood, demonstrated, was that this version was actable and could draw packed houses.

Lynchburg, STEPHEN SPENDER
September 26, 1979

MARY STUART

The first performance in Great Britain of Schiller's *Mary Stuart*, translated by Stephen Spender and adapted by Peter Wood, was given at the Church of Scotland Assembly Hall, Edinburgh, on 2nd September 1958 by the Old Vic Company. It was directed by Peter Wood, the costumes and décor were by Leslie Hurry and the music was composed by John Hotchkiss. The cast was as follows:

MARY STUART	Irene Worth
QUEEN ELIZABETH	Catherine Lacey
HANNAH KENNEDY, *Mary's nurse*	Rosalind Atkinson
ROBERT DUDLEY, *Earl of Leicester*	John Phillips
LORD BURLEIGH, *Lord High Treasurer*	Kenneth Mackintosh
SIR AMIAS PAULET, *Governor of Fotheringay*	Derek Francis
TALBOT, *Earl of Shrewsbury, Lord Privy Seal*	Ernest Thesiger
SIR WILLIAM DAVISON, *the Queen's secretary*	Gerald James
SIR EDWARD MORTIMER, *Paulet's nephew*	Ronald Lewis
SIR ANDREW MELVIL, *friend of Mary*	Jack May
THE EARL OF KENT, *Earl Marshal*	Dennis Chinnery
COUNT AUBESPINE, *Ambassador from the Court of France*	Norman Scace
BELLIEVRE, *an Emissary from the Duke of Anjou*	Edward Hardwicke
O'KELLY, *companion to Mortimer*	Barrie Ingram
SIR DRUE DRURY	Jeremy Kemp
AN OFFICER OF THE QUEEN'S GUARD	Charles West
SHERIFF OF NORTHAMPTON	Brian Jackson

GUARDS, LADIES, etc. John Barcroft, Michael Danvers-Walker, Desmond Davies, Philip Elsmore, Martin Redpath, John Scarborough, Davina Beswick, Silvia Francis, Anne Iddon

ACT I

SCENE 1

SCENE: *A room in Fotheringay Castle.*

HANNA KENNEDY, *nurse of Mary Queen of Scots, discovered quarrelling violently with Paulet, who is about to break open a cupboard.* DRUE DRURY, *his assistant, has a crowbar.*

HANNA: What are you up to now? What new robbery?
Get away from that cabinet.

PAULET: First tell me, then,
How did this jewel come here? I see! I see!
Someone threw it from the room above.
The idea was to bribe the gardener
By giving it to him. Damn women's tricks!
Despite my supervision and sharp eyes
Valuables are still being concealed.

HANNA: Stand back!
These are the secrets of my royal mistress.

PAULET: Then they're precisely what I'm looking for.

HANNA: They're written in French.

PAULET: French!
Worse and worse! The language of our enemies.

HANNA: Papers written now and then
To while away her hours of prison.
Drafts merely, for letters to the English Queen.

PAULET: Indeed? I shall deliver them. Hullo!
What's that?
(He touches a secret spring and ₍akes jewels from a drawer.)
Valuable! You take that, Drury,

13

And put it with the other objects.
(He hands it to DRURY.*)*
(Exit DRURY.*)*

HANNA: Oh sir, be merciful! Don't take away
The single jewel she still has left.
The Queen can find a little solace
In gazing on the relics of her majesty.
What else is there you haven't taken from her?

PAULET: Nothing has disappeared. All's catalogued
To render to the owner in due course.

HANNA: Who would ever know from these bare walls
A Queen lives here! Where is the throne
Beneath the royal canopy? Must she set
Her delicate foot accustomed to
Soft carpets, on this floor of the bare earth?
Bare walls! Not even a mirror to give back to her
Her poor insulted image.

PAULET: If she could see that poor insulted image
She would still hope, and spur men on to save her.

HANNA: Not one book left to bring a little solace.

PAULET: She has the Bible to improve her soul.

HANNA: Is this a fitting place for one raised gently,
One who was Queen already in her cradle,
And, as a child, at Catherine of Medici's
Prodigal court, indulged in every whim?
Must you deprive her of this trinket?

PAULET: Trinkets incline the heart to vanity
When it should be examining itself
For inward cause of just repentance.

HANNA: If in her past, when she was young, she sinned,
Then she must make her strict account to God,
To God, and her own heart—not to the English.

PAULET: Judgment will operate on her transgressions.

HANNA: Transgress! How can she, so confined?

PAULET: Confined, you say! Out of this narrow prison
She still can reach into the world, to rouse
Rebel bands against the English Queen.
Did these iron bars restrain her
From drawing snares round Norfolk's heart?
The best

14

Head in the whole island fell for her.
Accursed for us, the day when England
Hospitably took her in.

HANNA: Accursed for her, rather, that day when she
First set foot on English soil.
A suppliant, driven out, she came to seek
Help from her sister. Instead, she was
Condemned to weep away her youth in prison.
That was the taste of English hospitality!

PAULET: She came here, a known murderess, driven out
By her own people from the throne she had
Dishonoured by her monstrous outrages.
She came conspiring against England,
Pledged to bring back Bloody Mary's days,
And give to France an England remade Catholic.
Sooner than renounce her empty title,
She stays in prison here nursing her wrongs.
And why? Because she still puts faith in plots
Made here, sent from behind these walls,
By which she thinks that she can conquer England.

HANNA: How dare you say that she has such ambitions?
No voice of friend can reach her from her home.
Here she has seen
No face except her gaoler's, till today
When your young nephew's come
To put new bars around her.

PAULET: There are no bolts nor bars
Strong enough to hold against her cunning.
How do I know that this floor and these walls
Are not burrowed hollow from within
To let some traitor enter while I sleep?
I do not trust the lady. I would rather
Guard hell's gates, than this contentious Queen.

SCENE 2

The same. Enter MARY, *veiled, crucifix in hand.*

MARY: Sir, what you hold

There in your hand, taken by force, I had
Voluntarily resolved to render to you
Today. Amongst those papers, you will find
A letter to my royal sister.
Promise me you will deliver it
To her, with your own hand, and not to Burleigh.

PAULET: I will reflect on what is most befitting.

MARY: These are its contents: I have asked
Elizabeth the favour of an audience.
I will see her whom I have never seen.
                     They have
Summoned me before a court of those
I do not recognize as equals. I mistrust them.
Elizabeth is my blood, my rank, my sex.
With her, who is my sister, England's Queen,
I shall be open.

PAULET: You grow particular. Before now,
Times enough, you have put life and honour
In less trustworthy hands.

MARY: I have another favour yet to ask you
Which you would be inhuman to refuse.
Many years I have been shut in prison
Without the Church's solace, the holy sacrament.
Though she who's robbed me of my crown and
    freedom
Hunts my very life now as her quarry,
I do not care to think that she would bar
Me out from Heaven's gates.

PAULET: To your petitioning, the dean will—

MARY: None of your deans! I ask
For a priest, a priest of my own church. Also
I demand secretaries and notary
To whom I will dictate my testament.
I choose now to dispose of what I have.

PAULET: Do what you will with what is yours.
The Queen of England will not rob you.
    (*He is going.*)

MARY: Are you going, sir? Will you leave me so,
The question that torments me still unanswered?
My agony of waiting has now lasted

A month, since forty high commissioners
Overtook me in this castle; set up
Their tribunal; questioned me
With cunning, when
I was quite unprepared,
And was allowed no lawyer. Then, like shadows,
As they had come, as suddenly they went.
And since the day they went, you are all silent.
I vainly seek to read from your expression
Whether my innocence has been established.
Whether I ought to hope, or to despair?

PAULET: You will get justice.
MARY: Is my case decided?
PAULET: I have no knowledge.
MARY: Then . . . am I condemned?
PAULET: I have no knowledge.
MARY: They like to work here quickly. Will my murderers
Fall upon me, as my judges did?
PAULET: You will do well to think they will.
MARY: Nothing decided by a court at Westminster,
Uniting Burleigh's hate with Hatton's envy,
Could astonish me. And yet I doubt
What Queen Elizabeth will dare.
PAULET: What justice will pronounce she will perform,
Be the whole world her witness.

SCENE 3

The same. MORTIMER, *Paulet's nephew, enters, and without heeding the Queen, addresses* PAULET.

MORTIMER: You're wanted, Uncle.
    (*He departs in the same abrupt manner.*
      The QUEEN *observes this behaviour with annoyance and turns to* PAULET *who's about to follow his nephew.*)
MARY: Sir, one more plea,
I endure much

Out of respect for your old age.
The impertinence of this youth I will not tolerate.
Spare me further sight of him.

PAULET: Admittedly he's no soft fool
Melting beguiled at a false woman's tears.
He's well travelled, home from Rheims and Paris
And brings back with him his sound English heart.
Lady, I fear your arts are wasted on him.

SCENE 4

The same. MARY *and* HANNA.

HANNA: How dare he speak to you like that?
MARY: Oh Hanna,
We were too willing in our days of greatness
To listen to the flatterer's silver tongue.
How just it is, good Hanna, that today
We have to hear the accents of dour blame.
HANNA: So meek, so spiritless, my lady?
MARY: Oh, Hanna, shadows rise up from the past!
Do you not see what moves along the wall?
My king and husband Darnley, drenched in
    blood!
He never will make peace with me until
The measure of my sorrow overflows.
HANNA: Don't—don't think of that!
MARY: My memory is precise in every detail.
Today's his murder's anniversary.
HANNA: You never murdered him. The others did it!
MARY: I knew! I knew! I let what I knew happen!
HANNA: You were so young.
MARY: So young, and so much guilt
For one so young to take upon her youth.
HANNA: It was another you who let this happen, not you
Yourself. You had been driven
Beyond the bounds of your own nature by
Your lust for ill-starred Bothwell. You showed
With brazen face your shame on public view.

18

You let your husband's murderer bear before him,
In triumph through the streets of Edinburgh,
The royal sword of Scotland.

MARY: Go on! Go on!
Finish your story! Say I gave
My hand in marriage to my husband's murderer.

HANNA: Your soul has not been lost. Should not I know
Who nursed you, brought you up?
Your faults were vanity, frivolity.
Giddy ways. Nothing bad. The ill in you
Was work of demons. Demons that
Lodge in the impulsive human breast,
Deceiving the responsive heart, and linger,
Wreaking havoc there a while.

MARY: Who's that?

(MORTIMER *appears at the door.*)

HANNA: The nephew.

SCENE 5

The same. MORTIMER *enters shyly.*

MORTIMER: (*to his* GUARD)
Go outside. Keep watch before the door. I must
    speak with the Queen.
            (*Exit* GUARD.)

MARY: (*to* HANNA)
Hanna, stay.

MORTIMER: (*hands her a paper*)
Read who I am.

MARY: (*to* HANNA, *who is hesitant*)
Go, go, do as he says.
            (*Exit* HANNA.)
    (*Reading*)
From my uncle,
The Cardinal of Guise.
'Trust Mortimer who brings this to you.
You have no truer friend in England.'
Is it possible?

To find a friend
In you, nephew of my chief gaoler
And my worst enemy?
MORTIMER: (*falling at* MARY's *feet*)
                         Oh, your majesty,
Excuse this mask of hatred which it cost me
Agony to assume.
MARY: Rise. I am amazed. I cannot leap
So suddenly from an abyss to hope.
Tell me of yourself, and how you came here.
MORTIMER: Your majesty, at twenty I was one
Brought up with the utmost strictness.
Already, with my mother's milk, I sucked
Hatred for the papacy. Then
An irresistible yearning for travel
Drove me to Europe: made me leave behind
The puritanical dull preaching pulpits of
My homeland. Without halt, I traversed France
Burning with zeal to arrow to my goal
—Italy!
It was the time then of the Church's jubilee,
The roads were shimmering with pilgrim bands.
Each image of God was garlanded. It seemed
All humanity was setting forth
To the kingdom of heaven. I myself was swept
Along with the great multitude of faithful
Until I came to the precincts of Rome.
           Imagine how I felt, your majesty,
When the dazzling columns and curved bows
Of triumphal arches, rose before me.
The Colosseum's stone immensity
Hooped round my eyes' awareness. The spirit
Of absolute creation took me into
Its miracle-producing world. Till then,
I had not felt the power of art. The Church
In which I had grown up, abominated
The pleasures of the senses, abhorred pictures,
Honouring but the incorporeal word.
Imagine how I felt, now, when I stepped
In churches into whose interiors

Music fell from heaven: whose walls and ceilings
Overflowed with multitudinous forms.
The heavenliest and the highest, actual here,
Locked in a frozen dance before my eyes.
I felt them present, fired with the divine—
Ave of angels, Christ's nativity,
The Holy Mother, Trinity descended
Earthwards, and Transfiguration
In light transcendent. I saw his Holiness
Seated on high in splendour, holding
Exalted office, while he blessed the humble.
Oh what is gold, and what the daze of jewels
With which the kings of earth adorn themselves
Compared with him, instinct with godliness?
His house alone is heaven's real kingdom,
Because these forms are other than the world.

MARY: Oh, I grow faint, sir. Spread no more
God's quickening tapestry before my eyes . . .
It overwhelms. I am ill, and a prisoner—

MORTIMER: I was a prisoner also. My prison door
Sprang open. And my spirit
Burst forth to greet life's generous day.
I dedicated myself to eternity,
And with great joy embraced the truly joyful.
They took me to your uncle, that great prince,
The Cardinal of Guise. That was a man
Steadfast in strong humanity and born
To his vocation of guiding souls to God.

MARY: Then you have seen the face of him who trained me
So firmly through my early youth?
Does he recall me? Oh, speak to me of him!
Is he the same great rock that guards our Church?

MORTIMER: A rock! And yet he stooped to save my soul!

MARY: So you are one among the thousands
He with eloquence a gift from heaven,
Grappled to him, and pointed to salvation!

MORTIMER: One day, when I was walking in his palace,
I saw a lady's portrait. Through the shadows
Her pallor shone like a white flame.
This face seemed haunted by unhappiness;

21

Yet through this suffering burned changeless joy.
The Bishop said: 'Well may you stand, struck
    silent,
The lady bears her sorrows for our faith.
The land in which she suffers is your home.'

MARY: So, I have not lost all, when such a man
Remains my friend in my misfortune!

MORTIMER: He demonstrated your lineal descent
From the House of Tudor, and convinced me
That you alone are she who should rule England,
Not this Elizabeth conceived
In an adulterous bed, whom Henry
Her father, himself named his bastard.
From this I learned that your just rights
Are the sole cause of all your unjust wrongs.

MARY: Yes, my unhappy and my most just rights
Are the sole cause of all my unjust wrongs!

MORTIMER: It was about this time that the news reached me
You had been moved from Talbot's castle,
And given over to my uncle Paulet—
Heaven's miraculous saving hand
I recognized at once in this event.
Plans were quickly made for my return
Here, to my home, where, ten days past, I landed.
How right they were, who buried you so deep!
The entire youth of England would rebel,
If Britons saw their Queen!

MARY: She would be well,
If every Briton had your eyes.

MORTIMER: Would that they might be witness of your sorrows!
I can no longer hide the news.

MARY: What news? Has sentence
Been passed? Tell me. I can bear it.

MORTIMER: It is pronounced. My uncle will arrive soon
With Lord Burleigh. Your two and forty judges
Declare you guilty. The Houses
Of Lords and Commons and the City of London,
Press for the sentence to be carried out.
Only the Queen hesitates, not out
Of human sympathy or mercy, but

22

	Through cunning. If she makes a show of waiting
	She hopes her hand will soon be forced.
MARY:	You do not surprise me. I expected this.
	I know my judges.
	I know what they intend.
	To shut me here in a perpetual prison—
	And with me, in perpetual dark, my vengeance.
MORTIMER:	Do not imagine that would satisfy them.
	Tyranny does not leave its work half done.
	Only your death can make her throne secure.
MARY:	She'd never dare to send me to the scaffold.
MORTIMER:	Oh, yes! She'd dare! Have no doubt of that!
MARY:	She fears the furious response of France.
MORTIMER:	She's signed a pact of lasting peace with France.
MARY:	The King of Spain would rush to arms against her.
MORTIMER:	She fears no king. She fears her people only.
MARY:	She'd never put my head on show for them.
MORTIMER:	England sends royal ladies to the scaffold.
MARY:	More than the acts I fear the devious means
	By which the Queen could rid her of a rival.
	I never put my goblet to my lips
	Without the fear that they will kiss the kiss
	Of poison, on the rim, left by my sister.
MORTIMER:	You need fear no longer.
	Twelve audacious young men of this country,
	In league with me, have this very morning
	Taken their oath upon the sacrament,
	By force, to abduct you from the castle.
	Count Aubespine, Ambassador of France,
	Knows what we're about, and gives his aid.
	The conspirators meet in his palace.
MARY:	What is this plotting? Are you not appalled
	At Babington's and Tichburn's heads impaled—
	As warnings upon London Bridge?
MORTIMER:	Babington's
	And Tichburn's severed heads do not appal me.
	The wager that they made which brought them death
	At the same throw, brought them eternal fame.
MARY:	Unfortunate infatuated boy! If there is

	Anyone who still can save me,
	That man is Leicester.
MORTIMER:	Leicester? The favourite of Elizabeth!
MARY:	Only Leicester. Go to him. Tell him
	Openly who you are.
	And as the proof that it was I who sent you,
	Give him this casket. It contains my portrait.

(She gives him casket. He draws back, then takes it.)

	Take it. I've hidden this so long
	Because your uncle's vigilance
	Barred every means to send it. Oh, you came like one sent
	By my good angel.
MORTIMER:	Your majesty,
	Explain this mystery to me—
MARY:	The Earl of Leicester
	Will explain all. Trust him. He will trust you.

(Enter HANNA.)

HANNA:	Paulet arrives at court, with a great lord.
MORTIMER:	Burleigh!
MARY:	It may be that already Burleigh
	Mingles his spies among your friends. Good fortune never came
	To any rescuer of Mary Stuart.
	Fly while there's still time to fly.
MORTIMER:	To die for you, would be to win a crown.

(Exeunt MORTIMER and HANNA.)

SCENE 6

The same. PAULET, MARY, LORD BURLEIGH

PAULET:	You wished for certainty as to your fate.
	Certainty is what Lord Burleigh brings.
BURLEIGH:	I come as emissary from the court.
	Your majesty, you have accepted
	The jurisdiction of the forty-two—
MARY:	Excuse me, sir, if right from the beginning
	I must protest. You say, I have accepted

24

The jurisdiction of the forty-two.
I never have accepted it. English law,
Is that the accused has to be judged
By a jury of his equals.
Who is my equal of your forty-two?
Monarchs only are my equals.

BURLEIGH: You heard
The articles of the indictment, and
You answered them in court.

MARY: Out of respect for these lords' persons, not
In recognition of their office.

BURLEIGH: Whether or not you recognize their function
As your judges, is a bare formality
Which cannot stop the course of justice.
Do you not breathe here England's air, enjoy her
Protection, benefit of her laws?
Well then, you're subject to them.

MARY: I breathe
English air in an English prison. Is that
Enjoying her protection, benefit
Of her laws? I scarcely know those laws.
I gave no undertaking to observe them.
I am not an English citizen: I am
A sovereign come here from abroad.

BURLEIGH: Do you imagine the mere title—Queen—
Gives you permit to foment in England
Civil War, when you are England's guest?
On what would our security be based
If the judiciary of England could not
Strike at the guilty heads of royal guests
Equally with her own traitors?

MARY: I do not wish to be exempt from justice.
I take exception to the judges.

BURLEIGH: The judges. Oh, the judges, how so? Are they
Or are they not, the foremost of this land
Whose independence guarantees their truth?
Chief of them—

MARY: —Pious shepherd of his flock—

BURLEIGH: Is the learned Archbishop of Canterbury.

MARY: Next?

25

BURLEIGH: Revered Talbot, Keeper of the Seals.
MARY: —Next?
BURLEIGH: Howard,
MARY: Admiral of the English fleet.
BURLEIGH: Tell me now—could the Queen of England
Deal juster than select from her whole kingdom
The foremost as the judges of this suit?
And although party bias might
Corrupt each of them individually,
How could forty-two such different judges
Be swayed by party bias to one verdict?
MARY: I am dumbfounded at the eloquence
Of one who never wished me better health.
How shall I, then, a poor unlettered woman,
Bandy words against your words?
Well! Were these lords as you describe them
I would indeed be silenced, my cause hopeless,
Quite lost, should they pronounce me guilty.
I see these judges you so recommend
Whose massive weight is poised now to destroy
    me—
I see these judges in a different role.
I see this high nobility of England,
Eunuchs suave in their seraglio,
Fawning before their sultan, my great uncle,
Henry the Eighth. I see this House of Lords
Just as subservient as the Commons,
Make statutes, and annul them, marriages
And then dissolve them, when the sultan
So nods. Today it disinherits
England's royal daughters, brands them bastards,
Tomorrow crowns them queens.
I see these worthy peers, within four reigns,
Under four governments, four times change faiths.
BURLEIGH: You say you are a foreigner in England.
You seem all too familiar with her sorrows.
MARY: And those then are my judges! My Lord Chancel-
    lor,
I will be frank with you, but you be frank
Also with me. They say you wish the good

Of England, and your Queen. They say you are
Incorruptible. Do not, then, confuse
Expediency with what is just.
I do not doubt there are among my judges
Many upright men. But they are protestants,
Zealous for England. They sit in judgment
On the Queen of Scotland, who's a papist.

BURLEIGH: I am not here to argue. The lawsuit
Is no more tossed on winds and waves of words.
By forty votes it is decided that
You have transgressed against the act
Passed by parliament a year ago,
Enacting namely: 'that if a disturbance
Occur within this kingdom in the name of,
Or in the interests of, any person
Who is, or may be, claimant to the throne,
The aforesaid claimant then shall be arraigned
With all the rigour of the law unto
Death.'

MARY: No doubt a law framed to achieve
My ruin, is capable of doing so.
Will you deny, my lord, you made the rules
Whereby you are the marksman, I the target,
And that you now take aim for the dead centre?

BURLEIGH: What was a warning you changed to a trap.
You knew of Babington's high treason.

MARY: When did I? Produce documents to prove it!

BURLEIGH: You have seen proofs enough, in court.

MARY: Copies transcribed by another hand!
Prove that the words were those which I dictated.

BURLEIGH: Babington declared before his death
They were the instructions he received.

MARY: Why was he put to death before confronting
Me with him, face to face?

BURLEIGH: Moreover,
Your secretaries, Curl and Nau, confirm
On oath those are the very letters
That they took down from your dictation.

MARY: Am I to be condemned on evidence
Extracted from domestics?

27

BURLEIGH: You yourself said
The Scotsman, Curl, was honest.
MARY: The rack could have compelled him.
BURLEIGH: On his free oath, he swore it.
MARY: Not to my face! How can this be?
Here are two witnesses, both living—
Confront them with me—let them
Repeat their testimony to my face!
Why do you deprive me of the right
Accorded common murderers? I have heard
That in this very reign, an act was passed
Decreeing that the plaintiff must confront
The accused in person. Did I hear wrong, Paulet?
I always thought you were an honest man.
Prove that you are so, now. Say, on your
          conscience,
Whether or not it be so? Is this the law?
PAULET: It is, my lady. It is English law.
I cannot deny that.
MARY: Well, then, my lord,
If I am treated by the English law
So strictly when that law constrains me,
Why is this English law evaded
When it might help me? Why, my lord,
Was Babington not brought here to confront me?
That was the law. Why, now, are not
My two secretaries, who are living,
Brought here to confront me, as the law demands?
BURLEIGH: That conspiracy is not the only one.
MARY: It is the one for which I have been tried.
Why is the law evaded? Answer!
BURLEIGH: It has been proved you were in correspondence
          with
Mendoza, the Spanish ambassador—
MARY: Why is the law evaded?
BURLEIGH: It is, moreover, known that you have schemed
To overthrow the religion of this country
And to unite
All the kings of Europe against England.
MARY: And if I have—I have not—but

28

Supposing that I had? I came here
A fugitive, entreating hospitality
From her, who is a Queen of my own blood.
Pleading for refuge, I was seized by force,
Begging a home, was cast into a prison.
I am held here against my right.
Is then my conscience answerable
To England. Is it not my duty, rather,
To call all monarchs—in the name of freedom
Protect and save me, answer force with force!
Yes, for there is no justice, only force,
In question between me and England.

BURLEIGH: Do not invoke the dreadful rights of force,
Lady. They do not favour prisoners.

MARY: I know it! I am weak, and she is strong.
Let her use force then, let her kill me,
Build on my sacrifice her safety—
But let her then confess that she employs
Force, only force.
When she would rid herself of her feared enemy,
The scabbard out of which she draws the sword
Is force, only force.
Tricks such as these will not deceive a world.
Let her dare show herself before
The world, for what she is!
Murder me, she may, she cannot judge me.

SCENE 7

PAULET, BURLEIGH.

BURLEIGH: She defies us—will defy us always, Paulet.
To the scaffold's foot. She has a will
That is unbreakable. Did she tremble
Hearing the sentence? Did she beg for pity?
She knows the English Queen's ambiguous mind.

PAULET: There have been grave irregularities.
The plaintiffs should have been produced.

BURLEIGH: They never could have been. Her power

Of weaving spells and moving men to tears
Is still too great. If Curl, her secretary,
Face to face with her, was asked to say
The single word on which her life depended,
He would retract his evidence, be sure of it.

PAULET: And yet without that strict correctness
Where the procedure accords to the accused
Her utmost legal rights, our enemies
Will whisper up the world against us,
And our sententious show of justice
Will seem but sacrilegious blasphemy.

BURLEIGH: It is the fear of that which so torments
The Queen. Had she but died before—

PAULET: Amen!

BURLEIGH: Had but an illness struck her down!

PAULET: We would have then been spared this illness.

BURLEIGH: Our enemies would still have called us murderers.

PAULET: You cannot stop men thinking what they will.

BURLEIGH: No one will believe in woman's justice—
Least, when its object is a woman.
It matters not that we, the judges,
Pronounce from certainties. Elizabeth
Has her privilege of royal mercy.
She has to use it!
Opinion will not let her let the law
Pursue its course.

PAULET: And so—

BURLEIGH: And so she lives, you say. No! She must die!
This has to end. That is the thought
That robs the Queen of England of her sleep.
Her lips dare not pronounce her hidden wish,
Yet her eyes speak it and their gaze inquires—
Is there not one of all my servants
Ready to take from me this choice, of staying
Forever apprehensive on my throne,
Or executing ruthlessly
The Queen who's my own blood?

PAULET: That is the choice.

BURLEIGH: And in her eyes I read the bitter thought:
Had I but more attentive servants—

One servant able to interpret
The implications of an unsaid wish.
When they took this lady out of Talbot's
Care, and put her into Paulet's hands,
The intention was—

PAULET: I hope, sir,
The intention was to put the utmost trust
Into the cleanest hands.

BURLEIGH: Spread rumours
That she is weak, grows sick, sicker,
Until her name dwindles to such memory
As seems a shadow thinning from men's minds—
While your sound name stays whole.

PAULET: Not my sound conscience.

BURLEIGH: For God's sake, if you will not lend a hand,
Promise you won't obstruct whoever will.

PAULET: (*interrupting*)
No murderer ever shall approach the door
Of her whom God has put under my roof.
To me her life is sacred, not one jot
Less sacred than the Queen of England's life.
You are the judges. Judge then! Break the staff
And when the clock strikes, let the carpenter
Approach with axe and saw, construct the scaffold.
Sheriff and executioner, they all
May come, I'll open my gates wide.
But, till then, she's entrusted to my care,
And, be assured of it, I'll guard her well.
I'll see she does no harm, and comes to none.

ACT II

SCENE 1

SCENE: *The Palace of Westminster*

Enter ELIZABETH, *attended by* LEICESTER, COUNT AUBESPINE,
BELLIEVRE, LORDS SHREWSBURY, TALBOT *and* BURLEIGH,
with other French and English nobles.

ELIZABETH: (*to* AUBESPINE)
  Our sympathy goes to those noble Frenchmen
  Whose gallantry has brought them hither
  From over sea. I fear they will miss sadly
  The court of Saint Germain. I am not able
  To give them entertainment to compare
  With that of the French court, fit for the gods.
  A sober cheerful people, who, whenever
  I show myself among them, press around
  Crying their blessings—that is all I boast.
  The beauty of French ladies blossoming
  In Catherine's varied garden, would outshine
  Myself, and my poor hospitality.
AUBESPINE: The English court inspires the foreigner
  With admiration for one lady only.
  Yet she combines within her unique person
  All that enchants in all her sex.
BELLIEVRE: Grant us when we take our leave, great majesty,
  The single syllable that will make happy
  The Duke our royal master. May we be carriers
  On swift wings to his enchanted ear
  Of that *yes* from your mouth, for which he sighs.
ELIZABETH: Press me no further now, Count Bellievre.

This is no day to light my bridal torch.
Above this land the sky is dark with clouds.
Sombre mourning weeds would suit me better
Than bright magnificence of bridal robes.
A dire blow is levelled at my heart.

BELLIEVRE: Give us your promise only, then, O Queen!
And let it be fulfilled when times are happier.

ELIZABETH: Monarchs are but slaves of their condition.
They are not free to follow their own hearts.
I always wished never to marry
So one day men would read above my grave:
'Here lies the virgin Queen.'
But my subjects will not have it so
And thus they make it plain to me, for them
I am mere woman. Yet I meant to rule
Like a man, ay, like a king.
And I still think a Queen who spends her days
Not uselessly in vapid dreaming
But, uncomplaining, indefatigably
Performs the hardest of all duties—she
Should be exempted from those laws of nature
Which have made one half of humanity
The chattels of the other.

AUBESPINE: We know, your majesty, you have enhanced
Virtues of ruling. Nothing now remains
Except you should outshine, through your
        example,
Your own sex in their strictest functions.
It's true there is no man on earth deserving
That you should sacrifice your freedom to him.
And yet if birth, if rank, if heroic virtue
Deserve that honour, then . . .

ELIZABETH: I do not doubt,
My lord ambassador, that marriage with
A royal son of France, would do me honour.
Yes—I admit it unreservedly—
If it must be—if I have no choice but
Submit my own will to my people's wishes—
And I do fear that theirs will overrule mine—
Then, in the whole of Europe there's no prince

33

To whom I would more gladly sacrifice
My freedom. May this satisfy him.

BELLIEVRE: It is lovely as hope and yet it is
Hope only, and my master hoped for more.

ELIZABETH: What did he want then? (*Draws ring from finger and
contemplates it*)
In this, the Queen has nothing
Above the wife of any commoner.
The same symbol seals the same service
To the same subjection. The ring means marriage
And rings are links which add up to our chains.
Give his Highness this ring. It is no chain
And yet it could grow into that which binds me.

BELLIEVRE: (*kneeling and taking ring*)
Kneeling, I take this gift, and in the name
Of him who is my master, press my lips
In homage, to the hands of my princess.

ELIZABETH: (*to* EARL OF LEICESTER)
Permit me, my lord. (*Takes ribbon from his neck and
puts it round that of* BELLIEVRE)
Invest his highness
With this with which I now do honour you.
'Honi soit qui mal y pense.' Let envy
Disappear between our nations.

AUBESPINE: Oh what a day is this, made joyous by
Your magnanimity, great majesty!
I see such mercy stream now from your face
That I could wish one ray of that effulgence
Might fall upon a sorrowful princess
Whose fate is the concern of both our nations!

ELIZABETH: No more, my lord. We must not intermingle
Matters so completely opposite.
If France seeks an alliance seriously,
Then she will have to care about my cares,
And not be friendly with my enemies . . .

AUBESPINE: Oh how should France be worthy in your sight
If in this pact between us, she ignored
The unhappy sharer of her faith, and widow
Of her king? Honour and humanity
Alike demand . . .

ELIZABETH: France
    Fulfils obligations to her friend. I must
    Fulfil my different ones, to England.
    (She inclines to the French who, with the other lords,
    respectfully withdraw.)

SCENE 2

The same. ELIZABETH, LEICESTER, BURLEIGH, TALBOT. *The Queen is seated.*

BURLEIGH: Most glorious majesty, today you crown
    Your people's aspirations. Now at last
    We can rest on the blessings of these days
    That you grant us, without anticipating
    A future of tomorrows black with storm.
    Only one care still weighs upon the land,
    All voices beg of you one sacrifice.
    Grant us but this, and then today will write
    The opening of a psalm of English peace.
ELIZABETH: What is it that my people still demand?
BURLEIGH: The head of Mary Stuart. If you would give
    The precious gift of freedom to your people
    And make secure for them their hard-won faith,
    The head of Mary Stuart must fall. If we
    Are not to live endlessly apprehensive
    Whilst in the dark of Fotheringay castle
    That witch still conjures plots and tries
    To set this land ablaze with her love torch,
    Her head must fall
    For her, young men go gladly to sure death.
    They dream of freeing her. But what she claims
    Is nothing else except your throne.
    There can be no peace with a Stuart.
    She lives—you die. She dies—and you will live.
ELIZABETH: Yours is counsel of foreboding, Burleigh.
    I trust your pure intentions and your zeal.
    Your golden wisdom shines through every word.
    Yet I must loathe within my inmost being

The wisdom that calls out for blood.
Set forth some milder counsel, Shrewsbury.

TALBOT: May you continue to reign long, your majesty,
And may this England never seek to purchase
Safety at the price of her good name.

ELIZABETH: Why, heaven forbid that she should ever do so!

TALBOT: Well then, you have to find some other means
To save the kingdom: for the execution
Of Mary Stuart, would be to use foul means.
You have no right to sentence her to death.
She owes no fealty to you.

ELIZABETH: If it be wrong to say I have the right,
This is an error shared by parliament,
My privy council, all my courts of law.

TALBOT: Majority of votes was never proof
Of right. Nor is one English parliament
The voice of all humanity! Men's judgments
Alter, as do their tastes, from day to day.
So do not say to us you have to follow
Necessity, and your people's wishes.
You must judge, you alone. Have trust in
The voice of mercy in your inmost being.
God did not plant strength in the heart
Of woman. And the founders of this kingdom
When they decreed that women should be rulers,
By the same token proved the crown a pledge
Of mercy, not inflexibility.

ELIZABETH: My lord of Shrewsbury is an ardent advocate
Of England's, and my, enemy. I must
Prefer advice that puts our safety first.

TALBOT: She has no advocate. None dare incur
Your wrath, through speaking in her favour.
Pay heed to an old man with no more hope
Of gain upon this earth—pay heed, I say,
When I defend the one whom all abandon.
You yourself have never seen her face
Memory of which might light your heart to pity.
Not that I would defend her where she's guilty.
She planned her husband's death, they say.

ELIZABETH: It's certain

ACT II · SCENE 2

	After his death, she did marry the murderer.
TALBOT:	A dreadful thing! But such things happened
	In a sanguinary epoch
	Amid the bloody clash of civil war.
	She, a woman, and surrounded
	By oppressive carnal vassals, threw herself
	Into the arms of the most menacing—
	Who knows what devilish powers he used to win her?
	The will of woman can be overruled.
ELIZABETH:	Tell us no more of women's weakness!
	There are some stronger spirits in that sex.
TALBOT:	For you, unhappiness was a hard school.
	You saw the grave yawn at your feet.
	At Woodstock,
	And in the Tower of London's brick-built gloom,
	Your gracious father showed you grievous paths
	Of duty. No flatterer sought you out there.
	So unbewitched by the bewildering
	World, you learned control, and to distinguish
	Refined authentic values from the false.
	She was transplanted to the court of France.
	There in the endless round of revelry
	The earnest voice of truth could not reach to her.
	Her sight was dizzied by the blaze of vice
	And she was swept along the stream of pleasure.
	She was endowed, too, with the gift of beauty
	In which she outshone every other woman
	In loveliness of form, as well as birth.
ELIZABETH:	Collect your scattering thoughts, venerable lord.
	Remember we are here in serious counsel.
	Those charms indeed must be beyond comparison
	To have fired you, at your age, to such eloquence.
	My lord of Leicester! Only you are silent.
	What profound cogitations bind your tongue?
LEICESTER:	I am silent through astonishment, your majesty,
	At these horrific shrieks that fill my ears.
	To think that ghoulish tales which might alarm
	The superstitious mobs in London streets
	Should occupy such wise and earnest heads!

37

What makes this threadbare Queen so terrifying?
Is it her claims upon this kingdom?
Does not Henry's last will pass her over
Unmentioned? And would England, happy
In the revelation of new faith,
Revert to papistry, or substitute
A much-loved monarch for the murderess
Of Darnley? By God, I hope you will
Live many years to walk over her grave
Without the need to push her into it.

BURLEIGH: The Earl of Leicester once held other views.

LEICESTER: It's true that in the trial I gave my vote
For the death sentence. Here in council, though,
I must speak otherwise. Here prudence,
Not jurisprudence, is the question.
Is this a time to act from fear when she's
Forsaken by her one protector, France?
When you, now pledged to bring great happiness
To the king's son, revive your people's hopes
That you will bless your country with an heir?
What end is served in killing her? For she
Is dead already.
Neglect is her true death. Beware then
Lest pity trumpet her to resurrection.
My counsel is—let the death sentence stand.
Let her live on, but live
Under perpetual terror of the axe.
If she but raise a finger, let it fall.

ELIZABETH: (rising)
My lords, I have heard your views.
                    I thank you, all.
Now I shall ponder on your reasonings.
With help from God, who lights the paths of kings.

SCENE 3

The same. Enter PAULET *and* MORTIMER.

ELIZABETH: Sir Amias Paulet! Sir, what news?

PAULET: Gracious sovereign,
My nephew, recently returned
From a long journey, kneels before your feet.
I beg you to accept his youthful homage
And may he prosper in that sun your favour.

MORTIMER: (*kneeling*)
God save my gracious Queen.

ELIZABETH: Rise! I know that you have travelled
To France and Rome, and also lived in Rheims.
Tell me what plots our enemies are hatching.

MORTIMER: May God reverse the darts they aim at you.

ELIZABETH: Did you see Morgan, and that spinner of webs
The Bishop of Ross?

MORTIMER: I worked my way into the confidence
Of all Scottish intriguers, to inform
You of their plots.

PAULET: They gave him letters
Written in cypher, for the Queen of Scotland.
Loyally, he passed them all to us.

ELIZABETH: It has been charged that you attended college
In Rheims, and there renounced your English faith?

MORTIMER: I won't deny I went to that extremity
Of deceit, in your service.
(*To* PAULET, *who shows her a paper.*)

ELIZABETH: What is this?

PAULET: A letter to you, from the Queen of Scotland.

BURLEIGH: Give it to me.

PAULET: (*giving paper to* QUEEN)
Excuse me, Lord High Treasurer,
She was within her rights in asking me
To give it into the Queen's hands myself.
(ELIZABETH *takes the letter. While she reads it,*
LEICESTER *and* MORTIMER *speak privately together.*)

BURLEIGH: (*to* PAULET)
What can it contain? Vain complaints merely,
From which our duty is to spare
The Queen's compassionate heart.

PAULET: She told me of the contents. She asks a favour—
To see the Queen of England, face to face.

BURLEIGH: NO!

TALBOT: A petition is in order.

BURLEIGH: The instigator of a murder, one
Who lusts after the Queen's blood, forfeits
The right to gaze upon the royal countenance.
Whoever's loyal to his Queen will not
Support this treacherous proposition.

TALBOT: Should the Queen wish to grant it, will you then
Obstruct the gentle impulse of her mercy?

BURLEIGH: The sentence has been passed. Mary's head
Lies already on the block. It is
Unfitting for the Queen to look upon that
Death-dedicated face. If she should do so
Pardon must follow from her royal presence.

ELIZABETH: (looking up from reading letter, and wiping her eyes)
What is man? What is happiness on earth?
To what extremity this Queen is brought
Who started life with such proud hopes.
How changed her language now from that when she
Arrogated to herself our royal arms,
And had herself addressed by flattering courtiers
Queen of three realms.
This cuts me to the heart. Forgive me, Lords.

TALBOT: Oh, majesty, it's God who's touched your heart.
Obey this impulse sent to you from heaven,
Stretch forth your hand to raise up the down-fallen.

BURLEIGH: Be steadfast, majesty, and do not let
A praiseworthy human sympathy
Mislead you now. You cannot pardon her.

LEICESTER: The Queen is wise and has no need of us
To make the wisest choice.

ELIZABETH: Go, my lords, and we shall seek a way
To combine mercy with necessity.
Sir Edward Mortimer, a word with you.

SCENE 4

The same. ELIZABETH, MORTIMER.

ELIZABETH: (after regarding him in silence)

Your bearing is most spirited. You seem
To have self-mastery rare in one so young.
Fate beckons you along the path to greatness:
And she who says this, is an oracle
Who can accomplish what she can foretell.

MORTIMER: Great majesty, all that I do, and am,
Is at your mighty service.

ELIZABETH: You're well acquainted with my enemies!
The Almighty has protected me till now,
Yet I live ever trembling for my crown
So long as she lives who encourages
Fanatics, and supports their hopes.

MORTIMER: You have but to command and she will die.

ELIZABETH: Oh, sir! I thought I had attained my goal
But find that I am right back at the start.
I wished to lean upon the law's procedure
And keep my own hands undefiled by blood.
Sentence is passed. It must be executed.
Yet it is I who have to sign the warrant,
With my own hand, this hand.
You see I cannot save appearances.
That's what's so terrible.

MORTIMER: What appearances
Could taint the perfectly just cause?

ELIZABETH: You do not know the world yet. We appear
As people judge us. What we really are
Has no one as our judge. And so the fact
That I am right, will convince no one.
And thus I have to plan that my intentions
As to her death, shall remain dubious—always . . .
For deeds of such ambiguous aspect,
The only cover lies in utter darkness.

MORTIMER: You mean—it would be best if—

ELIZABETH: Oh, my good angel sent you here.
With you things are serious, you plumb depths.
Go on! Continue! Speak out, noble sir!
How different from your uncle—

MORTIMER: My uncle! Have you told him?

ELIZABETH: To my regret.

MORTIMER: Think kindly though

41

Of the old man. His white hairs make him cautious.
ELIZABETH: Dangerous deeds require impetuous youth.
MORTIMER: My hand is yours to use. Your reputation
You'll have to save, yourself, as you know best.
ELIZABETH: I will—
When will you wake me with the news—
Mary Stuart is dead?
MORTIMER: Count on me.
ELIZABETH: When may I sleep in peace?
MORTIMER: By the next moon.
ELIZABETH: As to your fortunes, sir, you must not grieve
Should my gratitude come cloaked in darkness.
Silence is golden. Secrecy can seal
The closest bonds, intimate ones, between us.
                    (*Exit* ELIZABETH.)

SCENE 5

The same. MORTIMER *and* PAULET.

PAULET: What did the Queen say to you?
MORTIMER: Nothing.
Nothing of significance.
PAULET: Listen, nephew,
You glide now on a smooth and slipping surface.
Princely favours entice. Youth yearns
For honours. Do not let ambition
Betray you.
MORTIMER: Were you not the one
Who brought me to the court?
PAULET: Ay, and wish
I had not done so. The greatness of our house
Was not won at court. Stand firm, my nephew,
Do not injure conscience!
MORTIMER: Whose conscience?
PAULET: However great the prize be that the Queen
Offered you, don't trust her promises—
What she commanded she'll repudiate
When you've obeyed, and she'll avenge

<table>
<tr><td></td><td>Your deed of blood on you, to cleanse her name,</td></tr>
</table>

MORTIMER: What deed of blood?
PAULET: Enough pretending!
I know just what the Queen proposed.
She hoped that lust for fame would make your
        youth
More malleable than my cramped age. (*Pause*)
Have you accepted? Have you? Will you do it?
              (*Enter* LEICESTER.)
LEICESTER: Good sir, permit me
A word with your nephew. Our sovereign
Is graciously disposed towards him.
She orders that the Queen of Scotland's person
Should be entrusted to him. She will hold him
Responsible for—
PAULET: Responsible—that's good
LEICESTER: Sir?
PAULET: Responsible for! And I'm responsible for
Keeping open my two wide-opened eyes!
              (*Exit* PAULET.)

SCENE 6

The same. LEICESTER, MORTIMER.

LEICESTER: What's upset him so?
MORTIMER: Is he upset? Perhaps it is
The unexpected confidence the Queen
Places in me.
LEICESTER: Have you deserved the confidence?
MORTIMER: That is a question I shall put to you.
LEICESTER: You have something to ask of me in private?
MORTIMER: Prove to me first that it is safe to say it.
LEICESTER: Prove to me first that I am safe with you.
Don't let my lack of confidence offend you.
I note that in this court you show two faces.
One of these must be false. Which, then, is true?
MORTIMER: I note that in this court *you* show two faces.
LEICESTER: Who of us will be first to show his hand?

43

MORTIMER: The one that has the least to lose in doing so.
LEICESTER: Well, then, that's you!
MORTIMER: Well, then, it's you!
Such an interested, powerful courtier
Could throw me, with a word. My word's nothing
Against such rank and such a much loved favourite.
LEICESTER: There, you're wrong. In all else, I am
Strong, it's true. In this one tender point,
Concerning which I have to trust your word,
A despicable witness could destroy me.
MORTIMER: When the all-powerful Earl of Leicester
Deigns to abase himself to make me
Such a confession, then I'm bound to rise
A little in my own esteem, and give
Him the example of my heart laid bare.
         (*Quickly producing casket.*)
The Queen of Scotland sends this to you.
LEICESTER: (*terrified, snatches casket from him*)
Speak softly, sir!
         (*He kisses it and gazes at it in speechless joy.*)
                        Sir Edward Mortimer,
Do you know what she writes here?
MORTIMER: No.
LEICESTER: Surely she must have told you?
MORTIMER: Nothing.
She said you would explain this mystery, why
Leicester, the favourite of Elizabeth,
Mary's enemy, one of the judges
Who voted for her death, should be of all men
He whom the Queen of Scotland hopes
Will raise her from the abyss.
LEICESTER: Tell me, then, why you yourself should be
A partisan of hers. What made her trust you?
MORTIMER: My credential with the Queen of Scotland was
A letter from the Cardinal Archbishop.
LEICESTER: I knew of your conversion. It was that
Which first awoke my confidence in you.
Give me your hand! I trust you, sir.
I see you are incensed because
My heart changed towards Mary. The truth is

I never hated her. It was expediency
That made me turn against her. For as you know
She was affianced to me many years
Ago, when she still had her throne, before
She gave her hand to Darnley. Yet, then, I threw
My happiness with her coldly away.

MORTIMER: Now she's in prison, and condemned to death,
You seek her out at peril to your life.

LEICESTER: Ambition made me grow oblivious
Of youth and beauty. I began to think
Mary's hand too narrow, when I might
Hope for the Queen of England's.

MORTIMER: It's well known
She set you above all other men.

LEICESTER: Ten years subjected to her vanity!
To every change of her despotic moods!
A top whipped to each trivial faddish whim!
Cosseted in one moment's tenderness;
And, at the next, thrust off with prurient
Disdain! Equally frustrated by
Her torrid favours and the icy turns
Of her severity! Surrounded by
Her watch of argus-eyed suspicions!
Examined like a schoolboy, like a servant
Bawled at and cursed—

MORTIMER: My heart bleeds for you!

LEICESTER: And at the end, the prize eludes. Another
Will rob me of the fruit of my long planting—
Not her hand only, all her royal favours.
She is a woman, and he's worth the having.

MORTIMER: He is the son of Catherine. He has learned
The arts of flattering in a famous school.

LEICESTER: So my hopes vanished. In the general wreck
I sought a plank to cling to. And my eyes
Turned back then to their primal hope.
Mary's image rose anew before me
Like the first rose upon the branch in May
Making all heaven jealous with her beauty
So fresh, so vivid—

MORTIMER: So pale now.

LEICESTER: Ambition melted; and my heart
Remade comparisons. Then I knew
What I had lost, and there, lost also
I saw her, fallen into deep misfortune,
Far fallen through my fault.
And hope revived in me again that I
Still might rescue and possess her.
Through a trustworthy intermediary,
I let her know of my changed heart.
And now this letter you conveyed to me
Assures me of her pardon. She
Will be the prize, if I can save her still.

MORTIMER: You have done nothing, though, to save her!
You let it happen! Let her be condemned!
Gave your vote for her execution!

LEICESTER: Do not imagine that I would have let her
Go to the scaffold. No! I hoped,
As I hope still, to ward off that extremity—
Until at last the means is found to save her.

MORTIMER: It has been found. And I am here who will
Release her.

LEICESTER: What are you saying?

MORTIMER: I will force Fotheringay Castle gates.
I have companions. Everything's prepared.

LEICESTER: Do your companions also know my secrets?

MORTIMER: Our plot was made without you, and without you
It would be carried out, except that she
Insists it must be Leicester she will thank
For rescuing her.

LEICESTER: Can you swear—for certain
My name was never mentioned in the plot?

MORTIMER: I swear it. How cautious, though, you seem,
You want to save the Queen—and to possess her—
You find friends suddenly and unexpectedly—
Yet you show more embarrassment than pleasure.

LEICESTER: We must not use force. The attempt's too dangerous.

MORTIMER: You are too cautious in a cause of honour.

LEICESTER: I see the traps and snares spread round.

MORTIMER: I see them only to rush through them.

46

LEICESTER: This courage is foolhardiness and madness.
MORTIMER. This caution is dishonourable, my lord.
LEICESTER: If we should fail, her fortunes fall with ours.
MORTIMER: If we should spare ourselves, no one will save her.
LEICESTER: You'll spoil the plans I had laid down so carefully.
MORTIMER: What have you done at all till now to save her?
Supposing I were criminal enough
To murder her, as the Queen just proposed,
How then would you protect her?
LEICESTER: (astounded)
The Queen asked you to murder her?
MORTIMER: She mistook my intentions, just as Mary Stuart
Did yours.
LEICESTER: And you agreed to do it?
MORTIMER: To prevent her making use of
Some other hand, I offered mine.
LEICESTER: That gives us breathing space.
Relying on your murderous mission, she
Will leave the warrant unsigned. We gain time.
MORTIMER: We lose time, you mean.
LEICESTER: Perhaps I'll find it possible,
To cause her to confront her adversary,
And that step taken, it will tie her hands.
Counting on you, she will be willing
To make a show of mercy to the world.
Burleigh is right. If she should once see Mary
Sentence of death cannot be carried out.
MORTIMER: And gain what thereby? Her mildest prospect
Will still be a perpetual prison.
This has to end with one bold deed.
Why not begin with one bold deed this end?
Mary has many friends in hiding.
Be finished with pretence. Be forthright.
You are—aren't you?—
Master of the Queen of England's person?
Well then—command her to your castle—she
Has followed you there times enough—and show
Which of you is the man. Be master! Hold her
Under lock and key, till she frees Mary.
LEICESTER: Have you seen how this woman ties us

All to her apron strings? Seek out the heroes
Who led us once. You'll find them closeted
By their royal mistress. Follow my guidance.
Do not be imprudent—
ELIZABETH: *(off)*
Leicester—
MORTIMER: Mary still hopes
Must I go empty handed back to her?
LEICESTER: Take her my vows of everlasting love.
MORTIMER: Send them yourself. I offered you my aid,
Not to be your cupid bearing messages.

SCENE 7

The same. ELIZABETH, LEICESTER.

ELIZABETH: Why do you sigh?
LEICESTER: At this vision of you!
I never saw you look so beautiful.
I stand here blinded by your loveliness.
That sudden glimpse of you when you appeared,
Renewed the pangs of my impending loss.
ELIZABETH: Loss? What loss?
LEICESTER: Your loved and loving self.
Soon you will achieve your happiness
In the pulsing arms of the young bridegroom
Who will possess your unshared heart.
His blood is royal, mine is not, and yet
There is not in the whole world anywhere
One whose worship of you equals mine.
ELIZABETH: Pity me, Robin, do not blame me, that I
Cannot consult my heart. It would have chosen
Far otherwise. Ah, how I envy
Other women, who enjoy that happiness
Which would be mine if I could set
The crown upon the head of him who is
Dearer to me than all. Mary had it!
Oh yes, she let her hand follow her heart!
Permitted herself everything! Yes, she

48

Drank deeply of the cup of pleasure!
LEICESTER: And now she drinks the bitter dregs of pain.
ELIZABETH: She took no notice of men's judgments.
The world lay light on her, she never bore
This yoke of duties which so weighs on me.
But I put royal obligations first.
Yet it is she whom all the men prefer
Because she strove only to be a woman,
So young and old alike buzzed round her.
Was not decrepit Talbot even
Rejuvenated, speaking of her beauty?
LEICESTER: The Earl of Shrewsbury was once her warder.
She won him with her cunning flattery.
ELIZABETH: How often I have had to listen to
Men praise her features! What should I believe?
Paintings flatter and descriptions lie.
All one can trust is one's own eyes.
Is it true, then, that she's so beautiful?
LEICESTER: I won't deny I've often wished myself
The pleasure—could it happen quite in secret—
Of seeing Mary Stuart and you together.
Then for the first time you would really taste
Your absolute triumph! She'd deserve the shame
Of seeing herself with her own eyes—made sharp,
Of course, by envy—so outshone: as much
In physical beauty as in princely virtue.
ELIZABETH: In years, she is the younger!
LEICESTER: Younger!
Not that one notices. True, though, her sufferings
May well have made her old before her time.
What would make her ailing still more bitter
Would be to see you as a bride.
ELIZABETH: I have been pressed to grant an interview.
LEICESTER: Asked
As favour, grant as punishment. Even
The scaffold cannot so humiliate her
As witnessing her life foiled by your radiance.
That way you'll really kill her, just as she
Wanted to murder you.
Yes! Now I see

49

You never were so armed to win the battle
Of beauty as today. Myself
You fenced round with a pallisade of rays
When you entered this room. If you,
Now at this instant, as you are, appeared
Before her, it would be your proudest victory.

ELIZABETH: Now—no—no—not at this instant, Robin.
I have to think the matter over carefully.
I must ask Burleigh.

LEICESTER: Burleigh!
He only thinks of your use to the State.
Your womanly feelings also have their rights
Of whose finesse you must be your own judge,
And not these politicians. Yet, seeing Mary
Would be a subtle policy, cunningly
To win the people. At your leisure, later,
You could rid yourself of the opponent.

ELIZABETH: It might not be appropriate to look on
My sister in her need. They tell me
That she is not attended like a Queen.
Her misery might strike as a reproach.

LEICESTER: You do not have to stare into a prison.
Hear my advice. Today the court will hunt
Upon the chase that leads by Fotheringay.
Mary Stuart can walk out in the park
And you can go there accidentally.
Nothing need appear premeditated.
And if you are unwilling, you need say
Nothing, nothing to her, nothing at all.

ELIZABETH: I do not know whether I want to see her,
But you have said you want to see us meet.
Today I cannot cross your slightest whim.
Yet if I choose to do this for your sake
It well may prove, I warn you, your mistake.

ACT III

SCENE 1

Neighbourhood of a park. Many trees in front, a wide view in background.
MARY, running, hides behind a tree. HANNA follows slowly.

HANNA: You run so fast. I can't catch up.
                    Oh, wait for me. Wait. Please wait.

MARY: Let me enjoy my new freedom, run wild
                    Across the bright carpet of grass, like a child.
                    Is it true? From my grave have I really arisen?
                    Does it hold me no more, that dark gulf of the
                        prison?

HANNA: Oh, my dear lady, your prison door, alas,
                    Has only opened a few inches wide.
                    You cannot see the walls from here, because
                    The trees have covered them with their dense
                        foliage.

MARY: Then thank, thank, thank those thick and friendly
                        trees
                    That hide my prison from me with their density.
                    Here where I am only the sky surrounds.
                    My vision, no more locked in narrow bounds,
                    Can voyage where it will through space.
                    These clouds which the wind drives southward
                    Seek out that coast where France confronts the
                        ocean.
                    Oh greet that country where I grew—
                    I have no ambassador except you.
                    Where you sail in peace through your demesne
                    There are no prisoners of the English Queen.

HANNA: Oh, my dear lady, freedom so long longed for

MARY:	Has made your words extravagant and wild. See over there! A fisherman beaching His miserable skiff, could take me aboard, And rapidly row me to some friendly port. From the fish that he catches he scarce makes a living Yet tonight I could load his poor boat up with treasure. With one catch he could do what he never has done yet Haul happiness into his nets beyond measure, If his rescuing skiff would but take me upon it.
HANNA:	These wishes are all wasted. Don't you see Watchers on guard who spy on us from far? A sombre cruel prohibition bans Each touch of sympathy from reaching us.
MARY:	No, my dear Hanna. Believe me, I am certain My prison gates were not thrown wide in vain. This little favour is foreshadower Of our changed fortunes. I am sure. It is The active hand of love we have to thank. In this I recognize the Earl of Leicester. Little by little he'll unlock my prison Accustoming us each day to greater freedoms Until at last I meet him face to face Who'll strike my chains away from me for ever.
HANNA:	I cannot reconcile these contradictions. Yesterday they read the sentence to you. And suddenly, today, this freedom.
MARY:	Did you hear the hunters' horn? Did you hear it unwinding Its call shaking silver across the plain? How happy I'd be on my horse once more hunting Over fields in the spirited chase once again. Oh listen! I hear the echo that fills Me with yesterdays sweet and todays all of pain. How often a clamour like this has resounded Through the heaths of my homeland mountain— surrounded. The clashing hunt, and the tooth that kills.

SCENE 2

MARY, PAULET, HANNA.

PAULET: Well, haven't I done right at last?
Don't I deserve your thanks, my lady?

MARY: Why, is it you to whom I owe this favour?
You, really you?

PAULET: Why shouldn't it be I? I was at court
And gave the Queen your letter, as you asked—

MARY: You gave it to her! Really! And this freedom
Is the result?

PAULET: And not the only one, my lady.
Make yourself ready for a greater.
You heard the hunting horns?

MARY: (*shuddering*)
What do you mean?

PAULET: The Queen hunts in this neighbourhood.
She'll stand before you here at any moment.

HANNA: How are you, my dear lady? You look pale.

PAULET: What? Not pleased? Isn't this what you asked for?
Your request's granted sooner than you thought.

MARY: Oh, why did no one warn me?
I am not ready for this, not just yet—
What I had asked for as the greatest favour,
Terrifies me.

PAULET: No. Do not go away. You must wait for her.
Not that I do not understand your feelings,
Now that you will appear before your judge.

SCENE 3

Enter TALBOT.

MARY: It isn't that! It isn't that at all!
Ah, Shrewsbury, you will understand. I cannot
See her. Save me from having to set eyes on her.

53

TALBOT:	Come. Calm yourself. This hour will decide all.
MARY:	I have waited so long for it. During
	Long years, rehearsed what I should say.
	Now every word is gone and I feel nothing
	Except the burning sense of my own wrongs.
	My mind is filled with hatred for her—
TALBOT:	Restrain your wild blood. Nothing good can come
	Of hatred meeting hatred. And besides
	However much it be against your nature,
	You have to act now as the times require.
	It's she who's strong, and so you must be humble.
MARY:	Not to her! Humble! I cannot—
TALBOT:	You must!
	Answer respectfully, and throw yourself
	Upon her generosity, don't stand on
	Your rights, not now, this is no time for rights.
MARY:	I see that what I prayed for is my ruin
	And in my ruin my prayer will be answered.
	We should not have to meet each other—never!
	No good can come of it. I am too deeply
	Wounded, and she has too deeply wounded.
	Between us is what never can be healed.
TALBOT:	Before you say so, look into her face!
	I looked into it when she read your letter
	And saw how her eyes filled with tears.
	She is not
	Devoid of feeling. It is you who need
	More confidence. And for that very reason
	I hurried here to warn you of her coming.
MARY:	Is my wicked angel Burleigh with her?
TALBOT:	No one except the Earl of Leicester.
MARY:	Leicester!
TALBOT:	Do not be afraid of him. He does not
	Desire your execution. That the Queen
	Wishes to meet you is his doing.
MARY:	I knew it! I knew it!
TALBOT:	What are you saying?
PAULET:	The Queen!

SCENE 4

Enter ELIZABETH, LEICESTER *and retinue.*

ELIZABETH: Send back our followers to London.
     The people crowd round us too much.
     In this quiet park, we'll seek a little quiet.
     My subjects are too fond of me. I find
     Their joy excessive. It's idolatrous.
     Gods should be worshipped, not us humans.
MARY: No heart! Oh, God! No heart!
ELIZABETH: Who is the lady?
LEICESTER: Your majesty we are at Fotheringay.
ELIZABETH: Who is responsible for this? Leicester?
LEICESTER: It is an accident, your majesty. But now
     That heaven has inclined your footsteps hither,
     May grace and pity win their gentle victory.
     (*Trembling,* MARY *approaches* ELIZABETH.)
TALBOT: May it please your majesty, to turn
     Your eyes towards this most unhappy lady.
ELIZABETH: Which of you was it told me to expect
     A broken woman? I see a proud one
     In no way crushed by sorrow.
MARY: So be it! I will forget
     Who I was, all that I am. (*She turns towards the*
      QUEEN.)
     Heaven that decided for you, sister,
     Has crowned your dazzling brow with victory.
     I worship God who so exalted you.
     (*Throwing herself on the ground before* ELIZABETH.)
     But pray you to bend down in mercy to me.
     Do not let me lie here shamed, but stretch
     Your hand to me, your royal privilege,
     To raise me up from where I am down-fallen.
ELIZABETH: It suits you well where you are, Lady Stuart.
     I too give thanks to God that in His grace
     He has not thought it fitting I should lie
     There at your feet, as you do now at mine.

MARY:	Think of the changefulness of human fortune!

MARY: Think of the changefulness of human fortune!
Think that there is a God who humbles pride.
Honour in me, as you do in yourself
The Tudor blood that flows through both our veins.
Oh, do not stand so unapproachable
Like the sheer rock to which my wrecked hands
cling.
My life, my future, all of me, is here
Upon these words that seek to clutch your heart.
When you look at me with that gaze of ice
My tears stop, and my words freeze at the source.
ELIZABETH: What do you want to tell me, Lady Stuart?
You wished to speak with me. I overlook
The wrongs, as Queen, I have received from you,
And undertake my duties as a sister
In granting you this interview. Although,
In following a generous impulse, I
Make myself an object of reproach
To some, for having stooped too low.
They tell me that you wish to murder me.
MARY: You dealt unjustly with me, for like you I am
A Queen, but you made me a prisoner.
I came to you a suppliant, but you,
Against all rights of sacred hospitality,
Robbed me of friends and servants, freedom,
Exposed me to degrading misery,
Put me on trial before vindictive judges.
No more of that. I will eradicate
All trace of grievance from my memory.
How shall I speak about myself without
Upbraiding you?—and that I will not do.
You are not guilty. I too am not guilty.
I know! I'll say it was a dispensation!
A demon sprang up out of the abyss
To set hatred alight in both our hearts
Which were divided, even in our childhood.
The flames grew as we grew, and always men
Fed them with new hatred. Partisans put weapons,
Sword and dagger, unbidden in our hands.
You see, that is the curse fate sets on monarchs;

Who being divided, lay waste the whole world.
But now there are no others come between us;
We are together, you and I, together.
In what have I offended—tell me, sister,
And I will listen quietly to the end.
Oh, had you only listened when
I wandered through a world to seek your glance,
Things never would have come so far
To the sad meeting here in this sad place!

ELIZABETH: It was no dispensation, there was only
The black ambition of your house, the Stuarts.
There would have been no enmity between us
Had not your uncle, the power-lusting cardinal,
Who reaches out for crowns, besotted you
Into believing you could seize my kingdom.
Here even in this island of my peace
He blew up flames of civil strife.
But God was on my side, and the proud priest
Was driven from the field. My head
Was spared the axe, it's your head that will fall.

MARY: Now as I stand here in the hand of God, I stand and
swear
You would not use your force so ruthlessly.

ELIZABETH: And why not, Lady Stuart?
What is there that would stop me?
Your uncle gave
Example to the kings of the whole world
Of how to keep peace with their enemies.
He taught us on the night of St. Bartholomew.
I only practise that which your priests preach.
Why should our common blood, and your rights,
touch me?
Your church cuts loyal bonds asunder,
Sanctifies treachery, rewards regicide.
If I should free you now, where is the lock
Fastening the pledge that you might make me,
St. Peter's key would not at once unturn?
In force, my safety lies only in force.
You cannot make pacts with a race of vipers.

MARY: Oh, that's the reasoning of your dark suspicions!

You've always seen me as your enemy,
And yet, had you but named me your successor,
As was my right, then gratitude and love
Would have kept me, your sister, your true friend.

ELIZABETH: Name you my successor! Out there, are your
friends!
Out there your home, the papacy! Out there
The monk, your brother! Name you my successor!
Set a decoy for my life, and for my people!
Entrap our noble English youth in lies!
Turn their hearts back from new found truth!

MARY: Then I am only Mary Stuart's shadow.
Greatness no longer summons me, and you
Have wrecked my being in my blood.
Go reign in peace.
And renounce all claim upon this kingdom.
Let's make an end here, sister! Only say
The words that brought you here.
Say: 'Mary, you are free. Now that you've learned
My strength, learn of my generosity.'
Say this, and I'll receive it like a balm—
Life, freedom, from your hand. I wait. I wait.

ELIZABETH: And so you finally know you are defeated?
Have you abandoned plotting? Is no murder
In preparation? Will no adventurer
Stake all to be the sad knight of your cause?
—Yes, all is over, Lady Stuart. You no longer
Persecute me. And the world has other cares.
No one at this instant lusts to be
Your fourth husband, for you kill your rescuers
As you killed husbands.

MARY: Sister! Sister!
Oh God, grant me patience.

ELIZABETH: My Lord of Leicester, look now on the charms
Of her no man could gaze upon unscathed.
Well, well, your fame was won quite cheaply.
To gain the general favour cost you nothing,
You chose to make your favours general.

MARY: Oh—

ELIZABETH: Look, look, Leicester, now she shows

Her true face as it is. Till now we've seen
Only the mask.

MARY: I was guilty in my youth of many follies
When in my weakness I let strength seduce me
But with a royal open-mindedness
I did not hide my sinful deeds behind
The false show of a virtuous-seeming face.
The world knows what was worst in me, and I
Am better, then, I think, than the world knows.
But you, alas for you, when futures will
Tear off the unctuous superfice that hides
The hot equator of your stolen lusts.
You cannot be said to have inherited
Virtue from your mother. We know what vices
Caused Anne Boleyn to mount the scaffold.

TALBOT: Oh merciful God! That it should come to this!
Is this your self-control, your patience,
Lady Mary?

MARY: Patience! Self-control!
I have borne what is tolerable. Now let
My indignation so long sepulchred,
Spring from its grave! And you,
Who could teach to the basilisk
Its murderous glance, let my tongue learn from
you
To dart forth venom!

TALBOT: She is beside herself!
Ignore this madness!

(ELIZABETH, *speechless with rage, stares at* MARY.)

MARY: England is
Ruled by a bastard, and a noble people
Corrupted by a cunning trickster!
If there were justice, it is she
Who'd kneel to me, and I'd stand where she is!

(*Exit* ELIZABETH *and* FOLLOWERS.)

SCENE 5

MARY, HANNA.

MARY: At last, at last,
After the years of ignominy, the moment
Of my revenge, my triumph! She goes!
She carries death within her heart!
HANNA: You've wounded your inexorable foe—it's true
But it is she, who's Queen, who hurls the thunder!
And you insulted her before her favourite!
MARY: Yes! Humbled her before the eyes of Leicester!
He saw it, he was witness of my triumph.
And when I put her down from her high place
He stood near by, his presence gave me strength.

SCENE 6

Enter MORTIMER.

HANNA: Oh, sir, now all our hopes are ended.
MARY: Go, Hanna.
                          (*Exit* HANNA. *To* MORTIMER.)
You spoke to Leicester,
Delivered him my letter and my portrait?
Tell me quickly, sir!
MORTIMER: You won. You trod her in the dust.
You showed you were the Queen, she the im-
          poster.
A royal rage transformed your features.
You are the loveliest woman on this earth!
MARY: What did my lord reply? What can I hope?
MORTIMER: Hope nothing of the man. Despise, forget him.
MARY: You never gave my letter to him!
MORTIMER: What can he do? And what has to be done!
I will save you.
MARY: Alas, how can you?
MORTIMER: Now hope is lost, the paths to mercy blocked.

Actions are needed, courage will decide,
And everything for everything be wagered.
You must be saved before tomorrow.

MARY: What are you saying? Tonight? How is that
possible?

MORTIMER: I've assembled
In a hidden chapel all my comrades.
A priest was there to hear us each confess,
Who granted absolution for our sins
Past, and to come. Then we received
The last sacrament before our final journey.

MARY: What sombre preparations!

MORTIMER: Tonight we storm the castle. We shall murder
The guards, abduct you from your room by force.
So no one may survive to tell the story
We must kill everyone.

MARY: And Paulet? Drury?

MORTIMER: They'll be the first
I stab with my own dagger.

MARY: Stab your uncle?
Your second father?

MORTIMER: With my own hand.
And even though I have to kill the Queen,
I've sworn to do so, on the Host.

MARY: No blood must be shed for my sake.

MORTIMER: What, weigh their lives and mine against
My love for you? This is the moment
With you alone to which my whole life grew.
Death is but another moment after.

MARY: For God's sake, leave me! You are mad!

MORTIMER: I'll save you if it cost a thousand lives—
I swear by God I will—and that I will
In saving you, possess you.

MARY: Have you no pity, to see what you propose—
To thrust me from one hell into a worse?
Is it my destiny that those who love me
Should change to frenzied shadows, and arise
As ghosts of my dead enemies?
Must hate and love always conspire against me?

MORTIMER: Yes! My love, like their hatred, burns.

They want to cut this head off from these shoulders
Sever this neck that is so white and slender.
Oh, dedicate your body to my love
This body that is sacrificed to hate!
The crown is fallen from your head and now
You have lost all your earthly majesty.
Try! Raise your voice, call out for help and see
What servant starts up to your bidding!

MARY: Oh, who will save me from this rescuer?

MORTIMER: You made the singer Rizzio happy
And Bothwell found it simple to seduce you.
You trembled at him, and you liked the trembling.
If cruelty and terror are the means
To win you, I can summon them.
(Enter HANNA.)

HANNA: The Queen of England has been murdered on the
road to London.
Armed soldiers fill the garden.
(Exit towards house.)

SCENE 7

MORTIMER *alone.* O'KELLY *rushes in.*

O'KELLY: Fly! Mortimer, fly! All is lost!

MORTIMER: What's lost?

O'KELLY: Do not ask what. Think only of escape.

MORTIMER: I have to know.

O'KELLY: Sauvage, that madman, struck her.

MORTIMER: It's true then?

O'KELLY: True! True! Save yourself!

MORTIMER: The Queen is dead. Then Mary
Ascends the throne?

O'KELLY: Dead?
She lives. And you, and I,
We are the dead.

MORTIMER: She lives?

O'KELLY: Lives to take vengeance on us.

Go quick now!
The park is surrounded.
MORTIMER: Unhappy woman! How inexpiably
Your fate pursues you. Yes, you must die now.
And I you called your angel, caused your fall.
O'KELLY: Fly! Fly! And God protect your journeying.
        (*Exeunt in different directions.* GUARDS *surround and*
        kill O'KELLY.)

ACT IV

SCENE 1

Antechamber. AUBESPINE, KENT, LEICESTER.

AUBESPINE: My Lords, how is her majesty?
You see me quite beside myself with shock.
May heaven be thanked which so deflected
The murderer's blow from the Queen's body.
BURLEIGH: May it be thanked for having brought to nothing
The foul intentions of our enemies.
AUBESPINE *(to Kent)*
May it please you, my Earl Marshal,
To bring me to the presence of her majesty
To convey my—
BURLEIGH: Do not exercise yourself,
Count Aubespine.
AUBESPINE: Lord Burleigh,
I am acquainted with my obligations.
BURLEIGH: Your present obligation is to leave
England, immediately.
AUBESPINE: What's that?
BURLEIGH: Your diplomatic privilege protects you
Today, but not after tomorrow.
AUBESPINE: And what
Am I accused of?
BURLEIGH: If I should name the offence,
It could not then be overlooked.
AUBESPINE: My lord, the rights of an ambassador—
BURLEIGH: Do not protect a traitor to the realm.
LEICESTER ⎱
      ⎰ A traitor?
KENT   ⎰

64

AUBESPINE: My lord, think carefully what you're saying.
BURLEIGH: A pass, drawn up in your own hand, was found
In the murderer's pocket.
KENT: Is it possible?
AUBESPINE: I draw up many passes.
I cannot read men's thoughts.
BURLEIGH: The murderer
Went to confession at your residence.
AUBESPINE: I keep open house.
BURLEIGH: It seems, to England's foes.
AUBESPINE: I demand an inquiry.
BURLEIGH: Beware of the result!
AUBESPINE: My sovereign is insulted in my person.
He will tear up the marriage contract.
BURLEIGH: The Queen has torn it up already.
There will be no marriage now with France.
My lord of Kent, you are responsible
For the Count's safe passage to the coast.
The people, in their indignation,
Have stormed his palace, inside which they found
An arsenal of weapons. They intend
To tear him limb from limb if he should dare
To show himself. Hide him until their fury
Dies down a little. You are answerable.
AUBESPINE: And I shall gladly take leave of this country
Where privilege is trampled on, and treaties
Torn up. My King will seek revenge!
BURLEIGH: Let him
Come here, and find it!
(*Exeunt* KENT *and* AUBESPINE.)

SCENE 2

LEICESTER, BURLEIGH.

LEICESTER: Now you are in your element, my lord,
We all know Burleigh's pursed and cryptic look
When he is on the track of traitors.

Soon you will have a court of inquisition.
Words and looks will all be carefully weighed,
And even secret thoughts thrown in the scales.
And you will be the man on whom all hangs,
A frowning Atlas shouldering all England—
BURLEIGH: In you, my lord, I must salute my master.
For such a victory as your eloquence
Recently gained, I never could have carried.
LEICESTER: What victory, my lord?
BURLEIGH: It was you, wasn't it,
Who found behind my back the means to lure
The Queen to Fotheringay?
LEICESTER: Behind your back?
When did my actions ever shy away
From your great front?
BURLEIGH: You mean, it was the Queen
Who made you go to Fotheringay? Not you
Who took her there? The Queen asked you to go?
LEICESTER: What are you hinting at, my lord?
BURLEIGH: Only
The noble role you let the Queen play there!
The lofty triumph you prepared for her
Who innocently put her trust in you!
This was the magnanimity and mercy
You recommended to the Queen in counsel!
For this, Mary Stuart became a weak
Despicable opponent, whose poor blood
Was scarcely worth the trouble of the shedding!
A fine plan! Finely pointed! A shame though
The point was ground so fine, it snapped!
LEICESTER: If you have an accusation
Make it to the Queen, before the throne!
BURLEIGH: We shall meet there—and look well, my lord,
That your eloquence then does not fail you.
      (*Exit* BURLEIGH.)

SCENE 3

LEICESTER, MORTIMER.

MORTIMER. Leicester! You here!
LEICESTER: You! What do you want?
MORTIMER: They're on our tracks,
On yours, on mine. Be careful!
LEICESTER: Go! Be gone!
MORTIMER: They know of secret meetings that took place
At Aubespine's house—
LEICESTER: Well? What of it?
MORTIMER: And that the murderer went there for confession.
LEICESTER: Why do you try to implicate me in
Your murderous dealings?
Manage them yourself!
MORTIMER: Listen only!
LEICESTER: Why do you hang on me like a sick shadow
Around my heels? Away! I do not know you!
MORTIMER: Your movements also were betrayed!
Lord Burleigh went to Fotheringay. A search
Through Mary's room was made, and there they
    found—
LEICESTER: What did they find?
MORTIMER: A letter begun to you.
Exhorting you to keep your word,
Renewing your promise of her hand, reminding
You of her portrait.
LEICESTER: Devil take him!
MORTIMER: Lord Burleigh has the letter!
LEICESTER: Has he now!
MORTIMER: Seize on the moment! Be the first to speak!
Save yourself, and her. Accept some blame,
To avert worse. For I can now do nothing,
My comrades are all scattered, our whole band
Scattered. I shall press on to Scotland
There to seek out new friends. It's now your turn.
See what your reputation, and a bold
Front, can do.

LEICESTER: (*suddenly resolved*)
I'll follow your advice.
(*Goes to the door, opens it and calls.*)
Guard, there! Guard!
(*To the* OFFICER *who enters with* GUARDS.)
Arrest this traitor!
(*To the* OFFICER *of the Watch, who comes to conduct
him to prison.*)
Keep close watch on him!
A monstrous plot has been discovered.
I go myself at once to inform the Queen.
MORTIMER: Who said that I should ever trust a villain?
He'll stride across my neck, while I lie prostrate.
And of my fall, he'll make a bridge to save him.
—Well, save yourself. And I will guard my silence.
I will not drag you down. For, even dead,
I would not choose you one of my companions.
Survival! that's the sole good of the bad!
Death and damnation take the lot of you.
(*Exit* LEICESTER.)
OFFICER: He's armed. Take his dagger from him!
MORTIMER: Traitors to your God and your true Queen,
As faithless to Queen Mary on this earth
As you are faithless to the Queen of Heaven,
And servants sold into a bastard's service—
OFFICER: Silence the blasphemer! Seize him!
MORTIMER: Mary, Queen of Scotland, I can give you
This one last brave example, how to die.
Mary, Queen of Heaven, pray for me
And take me to thee, where thy blessed ones live!
(*He kills himself with dagger.*)

SCENE 4

ELIZABETH, BURLEIGH.

ELIZABETH: To lure me there! To make a mockery of me!
To show me off in triumph to his whore!

68

BURLEIGH: I still am puzzled what the potion was
He can have used to take you unawares.
ELIZABETH: How well he understood my fatal weakness,
Made me the target of her mockery.
BURLEIGH: Now you perceive how justly I advised you.
ELIZABETH: Oh, I am greatly punished that I ever
Strayed for an instant from your counsel, Burleigh.
Whom shall I ever trust, if he betrayed me
Who always was the closest to my heart,
Him who I permitted at this court,
To play the role of master, and of King?
BURLEIGH: While all the time, he was betraying you
To this false, Scottish Queen!
ELIZABETH: She'll die for it!
And he will watch her die, and then die after!
I have thrust him altogether from my heart.
Yet was I wrong to trust him? Why suspect
A snare hid in the vows of truest love?
I am drained of love. Revenge is my whole being.
Let him be taken to the Tower. I'll name
Those judges who will judge him—hand him
To the most rigorous action of the law.
BURLEIGH: He'll turn to you, and try to set things right.
ELIZABETH: He—set things right? Does not the letter
Convict him? His guilt is clear as day!
BURLEIGH: And yet you are so gentle and so gracious,
His glance, his potent presence—
ELIZABETH: You do not think
That this might be a plot prepared by Mary
To separate me from my dearest friend?
Oh, she's a whore who is refined in tricks!
Suppose she wrote the letter just to poison
My heart against him whom she hates, and thus
Cause his downfall—
(*Enter* PAGE.)
PAGE: The Earl of Leicester!
ELIZABETH: Presumptuous! Say I will not see him!
PAGE: I dare not tell my lord that, and he would not
Believe me if I did.
ELIZABETH: My servants fear him more than they do me.

BURLEIGH: The Queen forbids Lord Leicester to come here.
(*Exit* PAGE.)
ELIZABETH: I shall never see him! Never! Never! Never!

SCENE 5

LEICESTER: I wish to see the shameless person, who
Forbids me access to my Queen.
ELIZABETH: Ha! What impertinence!
BURLEIGH: Bold, my lord,
To storm in here without permission!
LEICESTER: Impertinent, my lord, to raise your voice!
Permission! What! There's no one in this court
The Earl of Leicester has to listen to
Talk of permission and forbiddings.
Only from my Queen's mouth, will I—
ELIZABETH: Do not come near me, treacherous man!
LEICESTER: I do not hear my kind Elizabeth
But that great lord, my enemy, in those
Ungracious words. I make appeal to my
Elizabeth. You listened to my enemy,
I ask you now—hear me.
ELIZABETH: If you dare then—
Speak—and, denying it, increase your crime!
LEICESTER: Let this superfluous person first retire!
What I have to tell my Queen has need
Of no such witness. Go.
ELIZABETH: Stay! I command you!
LEICESTER: What does the third one mean, between us two?
I wish to speak with my most worshipped monarch
I stand upon the rights of my position
—My sacred rights—and I ask that this lord
Should vanish!
ELIZABETH: Such arrogance befits you!
LEICESTER: It fits me well, because I am well favoured,
Favoured by your grace, which gave me standing.
You set me above him, and above all!
What your love gave me, that, by heaven, I claim!

And know how to defend it with my life.
Let this lord go, and it will take two minutes,
To make you understand me.

ELIZABETH: You try to cheat me,
In vain!

LEICESTER: That braggart is the one for cheating!
I only wish to speak straight to your heart.
That which I wagered, trusting in your trust,
That I will justify, before your love,
There is no other court I recognize.

ELIZABETH: Villain, it is that court, just that, which has
Condemned you. Burleigh, show the letter to him!
Read, and be dumbfounded!

LEICESTER: Mary Stuart's hand!
Appearances accuse me, yet I hope
My Queen will look beyond appearances.

ELIZABETH: Can you deny that you have been
In secret touch with her, received
Her portrait, let her fix her hopes on you?

LEICESTER: She writes the truth. My conscience is quite clear.

ELIZABETH: That's all you have to say?

BURLEIGH: He is condemned
From his own mouth!

ELIZABETH: To the Tower with the traitor!

LEICESTER: I am no traitor, though perhaps in error
Keeping what I did a secret from you.
And yet my aim was loyal, to discover
The Stuart's secret, so as to destroy her.

ELIZABETH: A lame way out!

BURLEIGH: My lord, you don't imagine . . .

LEICESTER: I played a dangerous game, I know. Only
Leicester of all this court, would have dared play it.
All the world knows how much I hate the Stuarts.
The man who is distinguished by your favour
Dares serve you the bold way he thinks the best.

BURLEIGH: Why, if the enterprise was so well chosen
Did you keep so quiet about it?

LEICESTER: Oh, my lord,
Your tongue is like a dinner bell that tolls
Before you serve a meal of your good deeds.

That is your way. My habit is
First action, and then talking, after.

BURLEIGH: You're talking now—but then you have to.

LEICESTER: And you
Congratulate yourself on having saved
Your Queen. You know all. Nothing could
Escape your prying eyes. Poor braggart!
Despite your supervision, Mary Stuart
Would have escaped today but for
My intervention.

BURLEIGH: Your intervention?

LEICESTER: Yes, mine, my lord. Her majesty had put
Her confidence in Mortimer, revealed
Her inmost purpose to him, gone so far
As to entrust him with the mission
Of killing Mary, is it not so?

BURLEIGH: Who told you?

LEICESTER: Is it not so?
Where were your thousand eyes, that not one of them
Saw what this Mortimer had planned?
That he was a papist; sent here from Rheims to murder
Our much loved Queen.

ELIZABETH: Mortimer?

LEICESTER: Yes, Mortimer!
He was my intermediary through whom
I corresponded with the Stuart. That's how
I came to learn of the conspiracy.
This very day she would have been abducted
From prison: he has just told me so himself.
That's why I arrested him, why he
Desperate at the exposure of the plot,
Took his own life.

ELIZABETH: (to BURLEIGH)
How grossly you have let me be betrayed.

BURLEIGH: You say this happened just now? Since I left you?

LEICESTER: In my own interest, I am sorry
That his life ended so. His evidence
Were he still living, would absolve me quite

BURLEIGH: Knowing well
The deep sincerity of his intent,
I propose Leicester be appointed
To supervise the execution.

LEICESTER: I . . .

BURLEIGH: Yes. What better means could be devised
To free yourself of the unjust suspicion
That you were her lover than that you
Should be the certifier of her death?

ELIZABETH: Let it be so.

LEICESTER: My rank should free me of this sad commission
Which suits a Burleigh better, in all ways.
He who stands near to his loved monarch, should
not
Accomplish any task that is unhappy.
However, if the Queen requires it . . .
                    (*Exit* LEICESTER.)

ELIZABETH: (*as he goes*)
Burleigh will share the task with you.
Let the death warrant be prepared at once.

SCENE 6

Enter KENT.

ELIZABETH: What is it, my lord of Kent? What is
This uproar in the streets?

KENT: Your majesty,
A mob of people round the palace
Clamour to see you.

ELIZABETH: What do my people ask of me?

KENT: A rumour has spread through the city
That your life is in danger, and that murderers
Have been sent by the Pope to kill you.
They say that catholics have conspired
To rescue Mary Stuart from prison
And put her on the throne. The people,
Believing this, swear nothing but the head
Of Mary Stuart will satisfy them—

	Of any lingering doubt as to my conduct.
BURLEIGH:	You're sure he killed himself? You're certain You didn't kill him?
LEICESTER:	Unworthy thought, Lord Burleigh! Well, then, hear The officer who took him into charge! Sirra!

(*Enter* OFFICER.)

	Inform her majesty precisely of The circumstances of the prisoner's death.
OFFICER:	I was on guard In the ante chamber, when your lordship Opened the door suddenly and ordered me To apprehend this knight, on charge of treason. During the performance of our duty, We saw him fly into a rage, and draw His dagger—accompanying the action With gross calumniating of your majesty— Then, before we Could intervene, the prisoner plunged the dagger Into his heart, and fell to the ground, dead.
LEICESTER:	The Queen has heard enough, sir, you may go.

(*Exit* OFFICER.)

ELIZABETH:	Oh, what a sequence of calamity!
LEICESTER:	Who was it then that saved you? Burleigh? Did Burleigh warn you of the dangers Surrounding you? No! Leicester stayed Your good angel.
BURLEIGH:	This Mortimer died opportunely.
ELIZABETH:	I do not know whether to think you guilty I do know who's the root of all this horror.
LEICESTER:	She has to die! I myself vote for her death! My counsel was To leave the sentence unconfirmed Unless she took up arms again against you. That she has done now, and for that reason I say the sentence must be executed.
BURLEIGH:	That is your counsel?
LEICESTER:	The welfare of the Queen requires This sacrifice. And I recommend Her instant execution.

73

ELIZABETH: Will they force my hand?
KENT: They say
They are determined not to go away
Till you have signed the death warrant.

SCENE 7

Enter BURLEIGH *and* DAVISON *with a document.*

ELIZABETH: What is it, Davison?
DAVISON: *(approaching her anxiously)*
You commanded,
Your majesty—
ELIZABETH: What is it?
(Just as she is about to take the warrant, she shudders and steps back.)
Help me, O God!
BURLEIGH: The voice of the people is the voice of God.
ELIZABETH: Oh, my lords, who will tell me truly
Whether what I hear now is indeed
The voice of all my people always?
Tomorrow I may hear a different voice
That shouts with just this urgency—and those
Whose clamour now compels me to this deed
Will blame me harshly, when the deed is done.

SCENE 8

Enter TALBOT.

TALBOT: They want to hurry you, your majesty,
Stand fast.
ELIZABETH: Oh, Shrewsbury, they compel me to . . .
TALBOT: Who compels? Who can compel you? You are
the Queen.
Now you have to prove your great authority.
Order those rude voices to be silent,
And to refrain from trying to overrule you.

KENT: The shouting grows much louder. There's no longer
Any way to restrain them.

ELIZABETH: Compelled! You see how I'm compelled.

TALBOT: I only ask postponement. Now one pen-stroke
Can make or unmake all your happiness.
Wait.

BURLEIGH: Wait, hesitate, make no decision, till
All England is in flames, the enemy
Finally attains her object, which is murder.
Three times God intervened to save you.
Do not ask for a fourth miracle.

TALBOT: Oh, your majesty, today you tremble
Before the living Mary Stuart. It is not she,
The living, you need fear, it is the dead one.
Today your people hate her whom they fear.
Tomorrow they'll avenge her who's no more.
And you will very swiftly note the change.
Walk through the streets of London when she's dead
And you will see a gap of desolation
Open before you where the people now
Crowd, calling out their blessings: and this blankness
Will be the ghost of Mary Stuart beheaded.

ELIZABETH: Today you spared me from the murderer's dagger.
Why, Shrewsbury, did you not allow the blade
To take its course?
I am tired of my life,
If one of us who is a Queen must fall,
So that the other live, why may not I
Then be the one who yields?
God is my witness, I have lived
Not for myself, but for my people.
And if they think that happier days will come
Under a younger Queen, this fawning Stuart,
Then let them choose, and I shall step down gladly
And go to Woodstock's silent solitudes.

BURLEIGH: You say you love your people more than you

Do love yourself. Show it then! Do not choose
Peace for yourself and civil war for England.
Think of the Church. Will you now let this Stuart
Bring the old superstitions back again?
Once more the monk in power, the legate sent
Hither from Rome to lock up English churches,
And dethrone English kings?
If Shrewsbury saved your life, then I must save
What matters even more—the soul of England.

ELIZABETH: Leave me to myself. There is no human
Counsel or consolation in these matters,
Which I shall put before the highest Judge.
What he advises, I shall do. Leave me,
My lords. (*To* DAVISON) Sir, you stay near by.

SCENE 9

ELIZABETH *alone.*

ELIZABETH: Were I a tyrant like my predecessors,
I might have shamelessly shed royal blood.
But I must pay lip-service always
To the people: those whom jugglers please.
And yet no one is sovereign who has
To please a world. He only rules who needs
To ask of no one his approval.
Yet is that so? For is it not necessity
That rules the acts of tyrants free to rule?
Ringed round by enemies, only
My people's will has kept me on the throne.
The Roman Pope brands me with excommunica-
tion.
France betrays me with a kiss. And Spain
Builds her fleet to destroy mine at sea.
An unarmed woman, thus I stand alone.
I've covered up the blemish of my birth
In vain, for my opponents call me bastard,
And set up Mary Stuart as my rival.
She is the fury sent by fate to plague me.

Wherever I had looked to find some joy,
Some hope, this viper lay across my path.
She took my lover from me, stole
My bridegroom! Mary Stuart!
That name bodes all ill luck I've ever known!
With what contempt she gazed down at me then!
As though her glance could strike me to the
    ground.
Bastard, you called me! An unlucky name!
I am bastard only while you live.
When Britons have no other choice but me
I'll be reborn in wedlock instantly!
(*She seizes pen and signs warrant.*)

SCENE 10

ELIZABETH, DAVISON.

ELIZABETH: Where are the other lords?
DAVISON: They went outside
To quiet the crowd. The tumult ceased at once
When Shrewsbury appeared. 'That's he, the one
Who saved the Queen,' a hundred voices called
—'The bravest man in England.' Talbot then
Addressed the people, and in gentle words
Rebuked their violence, to such great effect
That they fell silent, and the crowd dispersed.
ELIZABETH: The weather cock that turns with every wind!
Alas for those who trust its giddy changes—
Well, you may take your leave.
(*He goes towards the door.*)
                 And take this too.
DAVISON: Your majesty! Your signature! You have
Decided then?
ELIZABETH: I was compelled to sign this.
A piece of paper, though, can decide nothing.
My name here cannot kill.
DAVISON: Your name,
Your majesty, under this writing,

Decides all, kills indeed. The words here written
Order the sheriff and commissioners
To proceed instantly to Fotheringay,
Pronounce her imminent death to Mary Stuart
And witness, at daybreak, her execution.
There's no postponement here. Her life will end
When this has left my hands.

ELIZABETH: True,
God has committed great responsibility
Into your hands. Pray earnestly to Him
That in His wisdom He enlighten you.
I leave you to your duties.
        (*She starts to go.*
        DAVISON *stands across her path.*)

DAVISON: Your majesty, I beg you not to go
Until you have informed me of your wishes.
Have I need of subtler understanding
Than interpret the warrant to the letter?
Or have you thrust this in my hands, so I
May press it into instant execution?

ELIZABETH: I leave that riddle to your clever wit.

DAVISON: Don't leave me to decide! Obeying you,
Your majesty, is all my cleverness.
You should not leave the shadow of a doubt
As to your wishes in your servant's mind.
My slightest error unforeseeably
Might lead to my committing regicide.
State your intention in the clearest words.
What do you wish to come of the death warrant?

ELIZABETH: Reflect on its name. Does not that tell all?

DAVISON: You want it put in instant execution?

ELIZABETH: I did not say so. The thought makes me shudder.

DAVISON: You wish me then to wait, and to do nothing?

ELIZABETH: At your own risk. You'd be responsible!

DAVISON: Your majesty, what will you have me do?

ELIZABETH: All I will, is simply that I should not
Hear of the matter, think about it further.

DAVISON: One word of clear command—that's all I ask.

ELIZABETH: I've said it! And torment me now no more!

DAVISON: You've said it! You've said nothing!
You would be generous to remember that.
ELIZABETH: Intolerable!
DAVISON: Have patience with me, please,
I have assumed my office only recently.
I do not follow the complexities
Of courts, and kings. I was brought up
In homely country fashion. Please, be patient!
Do not withhold the word from your poor servant
That would make duty clear.
(*He approaches her.*
She turns her back on him.)
           Well then, take
The warrant back! It is a brand that burns
My hands, when I hold it. Of all men
Do not choose me to serve you in this task.
ELIZABETH: Fulfil the functions of your office.
(*Exit*)

SCENE 11

DAVISON, *then* BURLEIGH.

DAVISON: She goes. She leaves me here, confused, in doubt,
Holding this paper. What can I do now?
(*Enter* BURLEIGH.)
Good, good that you are here, my lord.
You introduced me to this office. Free me!
I took it ignorantly, uninformed
Of my responsibilities. Let me
Return to that obscurity from which
You raised me. I do not belong at court.
BURLEIGH: Where is
The warrant? The Queen summoned you.
DAVISON: She left me, in a rage. Advise me! Help me!
Rescue me from this hell of doubt.
Here is the warrant. She has signed it.
BURLEIGH: Give it to me then!
DAVISON: I may not.

BURLEIGH: What?
DAVISON: She did not make her wishes clear to me.
BURLEIGH: Not clear? Here's her signature.
DAVISON: It must be executed, and it must not.
            What shall I do?
BURLEIGH: It must be, and at once
            Give it. If you hesitate, you're lost.
DAVISON: I'm lost if I act.
BURLEIGH: Fool, you're mad. Take it!
            (*He snatches the warrant from him.*)
DAVISON: What are you doing? Wait! You'll cause my down-
            fall!
            (*Exit, hurrying after* BURLEIGH.)

ACT V

SCENE 1

Same scene as room in Act I.

HANNA KENNEDY, *in deep mourning, is occupied in doing up packages. She often interrupts this work, through grief.*
PAULET *and* DRURY, *likewise attired in black, enter. Many servants follow them, bearing gold and silver vessels, mirrors, pictures, and other valuable things with which they fill the background of the room.* PAULET *gives to* HANNA *a precious casket with a paper and indicates that it contains a list of the objects which have been brought in. At this,* HANNA *sinks down with grief.*
Enter a serving girl.

HANNA:	What is it?
GIRL:	I was going down the staircase
	That leads into the hall below.
	The door opened, and I looked inside
	And saw—oh God—
HANNA:	What did you see?
GIRL:	The walls were covered with black draperies
	And there rose from the floor the immense
	Scaffold, covered in black, and in its midst
	The block stood, black, and on a cushion
	The axe, bright as a mirror. Round the scaffold
	People crowded, with eyes that longed for blood.
	(MELVIL *enters.*)
HANNA:	Melvil! It's you!
MELVIL:	Yes, loyal Hanna, it is I!
HANNA:	We meet again.
MELVIL:	After so long.

82

HANNA: A cruel parting.
MELVIL: And a cruel meeting.
HANNA: You have come, then, to—
MELVIL: From my Queen to take
My everlasting long farewell.
HANNA: At last upon the morning of her death,
They have allowed her what they long refused,
The visits of her friends. I will not yet,
Dear sir, inquire about your wanderings,
Nor tell you of our trials, since that far day
When you were taken from us. Oh Melvil, Melvil,
To think that we should meet again now, only
To witness such a dawn.
MELVIL: Do not let us
Weaken one another with our grief.
We need our firmness as a staff for her
Who starts on her last journey.
HANNA: You are wrong
If you imagine that she needs support
From us, to go to death. It's she
Who gives us the example of her firmness.
Have no fear, Melvil, Mary Stuart will know
How to die a Queen—
MELVIL: Did she take calmly, then,
The announcement of her death? I heard
 she was
Unready for it.
HANNA: She was terrified
Not by her death, but by her rescuer.
Freedom was promised us. This very night
Mortimer vowed to rescue us from prison.
Divided between hope and fear, the Queen
Waited for daybreak. Then, at last, we heard
Men running, and a sound of hammering.
Hope beckoned, and the pulse of life began
Irresistibly to reawaken.
Then the door opened. It was Paulet
Come to inform us that the carpenters
Had built a scaffold in the room below.
MELVIL: Just God! Oh, tell me, how did the Queen take

This terrible reversal of her hopes?
HANNA: We are not bit by bit released from living
But all at once within one moment comes
The swift transition from the life in time
Into eternity; and in that moment
God granted that my lady could thrust back
All earthly hopes, and with soul resolute,
Complete in faith, grasp heaven. Then
No taint of knocking fear, and no complaint
Dishonoured our loved Queen. But only, later,
News of Leicester's gross betrayal
And the unhappy end of Mortimer
Who'd tried to save her, brought forth tears,
It was the world of others made her weep.
MELVIL: Where is she? Can you bring us to her now?
HANNA: She spent last night's remaining hours in prayer,
And writing to her friends farewells,
And her own testament in her own hand.

SCENE 2

MARY: What, Melvil? Is it you?
So you are come to serve me at the end
When I am dying among enemies.
A sharer of my faith will be my witness.
Oh tell me, dear old friend, how has it been
With you since you were taken from us?
MELVIL: Nothing
Troubled me, but that I could not serve you.
MARY: Now you need weep no more. If there was cause
For weeping, that was when my days
Were burdened with my sins.
So now you should be glad. My fetters fall,
This prison vanishes, and my freed soul
Winged with light flies up to greater light.
Beneficent and healing, death approaches,
The serious guide who, with his sable plumes,

84

Cancels the ignominy of my fall.
Melvil, I will confide to you my last
Messages, to those who are my own.
I bless my brother-in-law, most Christian King
And all the royal house of France.
I bless the Cardinal, my uncle, and
Henry, my noble cousin of Guise.
I bless also the Pope—who will bless me—
And the most catholic King of Spain. All these
Are named heirs in my testament, and they
Will not despise that poor bequest, my blessing.
Melvil: I swear this to you in the name of all.

MELVIL: I will convey your wishes to them all.
(*Exit* HANNA.)

SCENE 3

MARY, MELVIL.

MARY: I have reached the frontier of eternity,
A short time, and I'll stand before my judge,
Yet I am still not reconciled with God.
I am refused a priest of my own church
And I refuse to take the sacraments
From the hands of a false priest. I wish
To die within the creed of my own church.
For she alone can bring me to salvation.
Where thousands do obeisance to their God
I only am shut out. The signs of grace
Do not reach down to me in prison.

MELVIL: They do reach to you! They are near! Have trust
In Him for whom all things are possible.
He who could strike the water from the rock
Can set an altar in these prison stones.

MARY: You mean, here is no priest, no church, and
        nothing
To be revered. And yet our Saviour said
Where two or three are gathered in My name,
There am I present in their midst.

What consecrates the priest as mouth of God?
The pure heart, the unblemished life.
And so to you, I'll make my last confession.
So you, though not ordained, are to me priest,
And may your lips pronounce my absolution.

MELVIL: Since your heart drives you to the truth so
       strongly,
Learn that God, for your comfort, can perform
A miracle. Here is no priest, no church,
No body of our Lord, you say? You err.
(With these words, he uncovers his head and, at the
same time, shows to her the Host in a golden bowl.)
I am a priest. To hear your last confession,
I have received the seven consecrations,
And bring to you the blessed Host, sent from
The Holy Father, consecrated by him.

MARY: That such a treat from heaven should be prepared
For me, upon the threshold of my death!
And you, who were my servant, are the servant
And sacred mouth now of Almighty God.
So I bow down in the dust before you.
Oh, like an immortal, charioted
Upon a burning cloud, or that apostle
The angel guided through his prison bars—
And in the darkness of the stone cell stood,
Heaven's messenger illumined—so you came
Here to my prison and you snatched me up
When every earthly rescuer had failed.
(She kneels down before him.)

MELVIL: *(making the sign of the cross)*
In the name of the Father, and of the Son, and of
      the Holy Ghost.
Mary, Queen of Scotland, have you scrupulously
Examined your own heart, and do you swear
To speak the truth before the God of Truth?

MARY: My heart lies open before Him and you.

MELVIL: Tell me what sin weighs heaviest on your con-
      science?

MARY: My heart was filled with hatred and revenge
Sinning, I hoped of God's forgiveness,

	Yet could not pardon her who sinned against me.
MELVIL:	Do you repent of hatred, and is it now
	Your wish to die at peace with your opponent?
MARY:	As truly as I hope God will forgive me.
MELVIL:	What further sins does your heart charge you
	with?
MARY:	Not through hate only, but through carnal love
	I have still more offended God. My heart
	Was harnessed to the man who faithlessly
	Abandoned and betrayed me.
MELVIL:	Do you repent of lust?
MARY:	This was my hardest struggle, but I won.
	The final fleshly bond is torn away.
MELVIL:	In this last moment of your reckoning
	What further sin perturbs your conscience still?
MARY:	A terrifying early deed of blood
	Casts up its shadow against heaven's gate!
	I let them kill the king my husband and gave
	My hand to him his murderer.
MELVIL:	Is there no other sin which troubles you?
MARY:	Now you know all the burden on my heart.
MELVIL:	Consider the proximity of God!
	Think of the punishment the Church inflicts
	On those who make reserved confession.
MARY:	May everlasting grace crown my last struggle
	With joy, for I have hidden nothing.
MELVIL:	What? You conceal from God the very crime
	For which your fellow beings have condemned
	you?
	Why do you not confess the part you played
	In Babington's and Parry's treachery?
MARY:	I am prepared now for Eternity.
	If I should stand before my Judge's throne
	Before the clock's hand point to the next minute,
	I will have made complete confession.
MELVIL:	Weigh well the matter. The heart is treacherous,
	And with a cunning ambiguity
	Perhaps you may escape upon the edge
	Of the word by which men name you guilty.
	Think well how no such juggling can deceive

The eye of flame that looks right through your
    heart.
MARY: I have called upon the princes of the world
           To free me from degrading bondage,
           Never in word or deed have I willed
           The death of my great enemy.
MELVIL: Then your secretaries bore false witness?
MARY: What I have said is true. Their testimony
           Will have God as its judge.
MELVIL: You go to the scaffold
           Convinced, then, of your innocence?
MARY: I do.
MELVIL: (*making the sign of the cross over her*)
           Then expiate your guilt through dying.
           Through the authority which that Power
           Has granted me, I grant you absolution.
           (*Gives her the Host.*)
           Receive this body sacrificed for thee
           As now, within thy body upon earth,
           Thou art mysteriously knit with God.
           (MELVIL *places the cup down again. At a sound from
           outside he covers his head again and goes to the door.*
           MARY *remains kneeling, rapt in thought.*)
           There still remains one bitter struggle for you.
           You must receive Lord Leicester and Lord
               Burleigh.

SCENE 4

Enter LEICESTER, BURLEIGH, PAULET.

BURLEIGH: I come, Lady Stuart, to carry out
           Your last wishes.
MARY: Thank you, my lord.
BURLEIGH: It is the Queen's wish that you be denied
           No reasonable request.
MARY: My will contains
           My last wishes. Sir Amias Paulet has it.
           I pray you to observe all its conditions.

88

PAULET: You may rely on that.
MARY: I beg of you, may my servants, without hindrance
           Proceed to France or Scotland, as they choose.
BURLEIGH: They may do so.
MARY: And since my body
           May not lie in consecrated soil,
           May it be granted that my servants should
           Convey my heart to France.
BURLEIGH: Granted.
           What else?
MARY: Send my sisterly greetings
           From me to the Queen of England. Say
           I ask of her forgiveness for my insolence
           And that I wish her a long reign. And that
           I pardon her my death with all my heart.
BURLEIGH: Well. Have you reconsidered my advice?
           Will you see the dean?
MARY: I have been reconciled with God.
           (PAULET *gives her his hand.*)

SCENE 5

HANNA *and other women servants of the* QUEEN *enter, followed by
the* SHERIFF, *white staff in hand; in the background, armed*
SENTRIES.

MARY: What is it, Hanna? Yes, the time has come.
           Here is the sheriff, to lead us to death.
           (*Turning to her* SERVANTS.)
           And you, my followers, I have entrusted
           To my brother of France. He will protect you
           And grant to you a second fatherland.
           My last request to you is not to stay
           Here in England, so the proud English may not
           Glut their hearts upon the misery
           Of those who were my servants. Will you swear
           Now, on the image of God crucified,
           To leave this faithless country, when I am gone?

MELVIL: (*touching the crucifix*)
I swear this to you in the name of all.

MARY: My faithful Hanna, take this handkerchief,
Which in our prison I embroidered for you,
Through long sad hours, inwoven with my tears.
When it is time to do so, you may bind
My eyes with this; that service will be
The last I have to ask of you, dear Hanna.

BURLEIGH: I am not able to permit it.

MARY: Why?
Will you refuse me this one small request?
Remember, I'm a woman. Who but my woman,
Hanna, can give me my last service?

BURLEIGH: No woman is allowed to climb the scaffold.

MARY: She will not weep. Be kind, my lord. I can
Vouch for Hanna's fortitude of soul.
Do not separate me from the friend
Who was my nurse and help-meet from the first.
She bore me on her arms into this life
So let her mild hand guide me to my death.

PAULET: (*to* BURLEIGH)
Permit it.

BURLEIGH: Your wish is granted.

MARY: Paulet, I have often caused you grief. I hope you
Will not think of me resentfully.

PAULET: May God be with you. And go hence in peace.

MARY: Now I have finished with this world for ever.
Healer and Saviour
Whose arms were stretched out on the cross
Stretch them out now,
To take me to Thee!
You keep your word, Leicester, for you promised
To lead me out of prison on your arm,
Which I take now. I wished to thank you
Not only for my freedom, but for that
Which would have made it still more precious to
me—
Yourself, your heart, the way to a new life
Of happiness completed by your love.
Kneel at the feet of your Elizabeth!

And may your prize not prove to be your prison!
Farewell! Now I have nothing left on earth.
(*Exit, following the* SHERIFF, MELVIL *and* HANNA
on either side of her, BURLEIGH *and* PAULET
*following. The remaining spectators watch her
departure then exeunt on each side of the stage.*)

SCENE 6

LEICESTER *alone.*

LEICESTER: She moves towards her death, spirit transcendent,
And I stay tangled here among the damned.
What life from heaven I have cast away!
What has become of my determination
To feel nothing, see nothing but my aims,
Look on with unmoved eyes when her head falls?
Did her glance waken me to shame?
And must her death ensnare me now with love?
No, that's too late. She's gone. You are earth-
bound
You must pursue your gross aims to the end.
Make your heart heartless, watch with stony eyes
Her death, so you may gain your shameful prize.
I have to see her die. I was sent here as witness.
(*He goes towards the door through which* MARY
*has been led, then stands stock-still, unable to move
further.*)
In vain! My eyes are dazed! I cannot watch
Her death! I hear voices.
I hear the dean admonish her. She interrupts!
Listen. She prays. It seems so loud.
                                        So strong,
Her voice. Now all is quiet. Quite still.
                                        I hear
Only a sobbing from her women. Now they bare
her neck.

The block is brought. She kneels down.
Lays her head.
(*He collapses, fainting, and at the same time a loud
cry is heard from below.*)

SCENE 7

A room. ELIZABETH *alone.*

ELIZABETH: No one here yet! No messenger! Will it
Never be evening? Has it happened, or
Not happened? Both terrify me, and
I dare not ask.
Leicester doesn't show himself, nor Burleigh,
They have left London. So it must have happened.
The bow is drawn, the arrow flies, it has
Met its mark. Not for my kingdom could I
Stop it from striking now. Who's there?

SCENE 8

Enter a PAGE.

ELIZABETH: You have come back alone. Where are the lords?
PAGE: My lords of Leicester and of Burleigh—
ELIZABETH: Where are they?
PAGE: Not in London.
ELIZABETH: Where, then?
PAGE: Your majesty, no one could tell me that.
Before daybreak both lords secretly,
And suddenly, left London.
ELIZABETH: I am
The Queen of England. Go. Summon me—no—
She's dead! At last I have some room upon this
earth.
Why do I tremble? Why does this fear seize me?

My cause of fear is buried underground
And who can say I did it? I shall not lack
Tears to weep for her, now she's dead.
　(*To* PAGE)
Are you still there? My secretary, Davison,
Must come immediately to see me.
Send for the Earl of Shrewsbury.

SCENE 9

ELIZABETH, TALBOT.

TALBOT:　　　　　　　I am here, oh great Queen.
Today, spurred on by fear for your good name,
My deep concern impelled me to the Tower,
Where Curl and Nau, Mary Stuart's secretaries,
Are prisoners. Once more I wished to test
Their authenticity as witnesses.
The Lieutenant of the Tower, who seemed
Perplexed and troubled, would not let me see
　　them.
Only with threats could I gain entrance.
　　　　　　　　Then,
What a sight met my eyes! The Scotsman,
Curl, lay on his mattress, hair dishevelled,
Mad-eyed, in torment.
When the wretch at last
Saw who I was, he threw himself before me,
Clutching my knees, shrieking, and implored
That I should tell him of the fate of Mary.
For a rumour of the death sentence
Had penetrated even those deep walls.
When I affirmed the truth to him,
Adding moreover that it was his witness, his,
On which she was condemned, he sprang up,
　　swearing,
And threw himself upon his fellow prisoner,

And downed him, with his madman's strength, so
    that
He would have strangled him, had we not
    managed
To tear the wretch out of the madman's grasp.
And now his rage was turned against himself,
He struck his breast with his own fists, and cursed
Himself and his companions. He said they
Had borne false witness, and the fatal letters
To Babington, which he attested as
Genuine, were forgeries; that he had written words
Different from the ones the Queen dictated
And that the devil Nau had made him do so.
Then he ran to the window, broke it open
And with a loud voice cried into the street,
Where a crowd quickly gathered: 'I was
Mary Stuart's secretary, and the forger
Of false evidence against her, a damned spirit
Damned to eternity for false witness'.

ELIZABETH: You yourself say he was mad. The words
    Of a lunatic prove nothing.

TALBOT: Yet
    The madness is itself a fact that points
    To further facts. Oh, your majesty,
    Let me appeal to you, don't hurry,
    Order a new investigation.

ELIZABETH: Well, I shall do so, since you ask it, Talbot.
    Not that I can believe my peers would have
    Made a hasty judgment in this matter.
    Still, to allay your fears, let this inquiry
    Be reopened. Good, that there is still time.
    The slightest shadow of a doubt should not
    Fall on our royal honour.
                (*Enter* DAVISON.)

SCENE 10

DAVISON, ELIZABETH, TALBOT.

ELIZABETH: The warrant, sir, that I put into your hands,
Where is it?

DAVISON: The warrant?

ELIZABETH: Which I yesterday
Put in your keeping.

DAVISON: Put in my keeping?

ELIZABETH: The people clamoured that I had to sign it.
I was compelled to do their will, I did so,
Under compulsion, and I put the paper
Into your hands, so I might gain time.
You know what I said to you—now, return it!

TALBOT: Give it, noble sir, matters are altered,
The investigation has to be reopened.

DAVISON: Reopened? Merciful heaven!

ELIZABETH: Why are you waiting? Fetch the paper.

DAVISON: Oh, I am ruined! An emissary of death!

ELIZABETH: What?

TALBOT: God in heaven!

DAVISON: Burleigh has had it in his hands—since yesterday.

ELIZABETH: Miscreant! So that's how you obeyed me!
Did I not order you to keep it?

DAVISON: That was not what you said, your majesty.

ELIZABETH: Will you give me the lie, you rascal?
When did I say—give it to Burleigh?

DAVISON: Never expressly in those words, but—

ELIZABETH: Scoundrel! You dare to twist my words, interpret
Your own idiot meaning into them?
You'll pay with your life for it should misfortune
Result from your abrupt officiousness.

TALBOT: If Sir William Davison did this
On his own authority, without
Informing you, then he must be tried
Before the Court of his peers: for he has made
Your name abhorrent, to all time.

SCENE 11

BURLEIGH, *and then* KENT.

BURLEIGH: Long live my gracious Queen, and may
All the enemies of this land
End like Mary Stuart.

ELIZABETH: Tell me, my lord
Did you receive from me the death warrant?

BURLEIGH: No, your gracious majesty, I had it
From Sir William Davison.

ELIZABETH: Did Davison convey it to you
In my name?

BURLEIGH: No . . . not.

ELIZABETH: And you acted upon it,
Precipitately, without knowing my will?
The sentence was most just, the world cannot
Reproach us with it: yet you did most ill
To obstruct the gentle impulse of our heart.
For this you are banished from my presence.
(*To* DAVISON)
A stronger sentence must be given you,
Who treacherously have overstepped your powers.
Take him to the Tower—that is my order!
—My loyal Shrewsbury, you alone I find
To have been right of all my counsellors—
From now on, be my close adviser.

TALBOT: Do not banish your true friends, those who
Have acted for you—who are silent for you.
Permit me, though, your majesty, whom you
For twelve years have entrusted with the Seal
To give it back into your hands.

ELIZABETH: No! Do not abandon me now, Shrewsbury!

TALBOT: Forgive me, but I am too old,
And this right hand has grown too stiff to set
The seal upon your recent acts.

ELIZABETH: Will then
The man who saved my life abandon me?

TALBOT: I have done but little.
I could not save the nobler part of you.
Live long, reign happily! Now your great
   opponent
Is dead. The Queen of England has
Nothing to fear, nothing.
              (*Exit. To* KENT, *who comes in.*)
ELIZABETH: Tell the Earl of Leicester to come here.
KENT: The Earl sends
His excuses. He has embarked for France.

CURTAIN

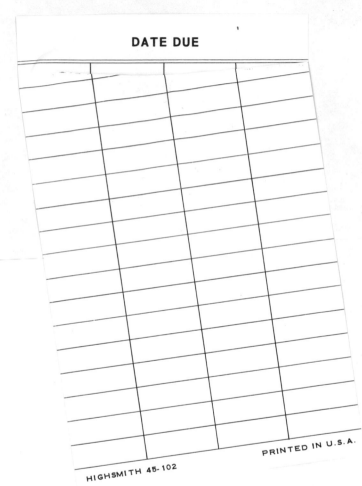

DATE DUE

HIGHSMITH 45-102

PRINTED IN U.S.A.